# The Progression of Human Rights: From Magna Carta to Modern Movements

Shah Rukh

Published by Shah Rukh, 2024.

While every precaution has been taken in the preparation of this book, the publisher assumes no responsibility for errors or omissions, or for damages resulting from the use of the information contained herein.

THE PROGRESSION OF HUMAN RIGHTS: FROM MAGNA CARTA TO MODERN MOVEMENTS

**First edition. June 5, 2024.**

Copyright © 2024 Shah Rukh.

Written by Shah Rukh.

# Table of Contents

# Prologue

Human rights are the bedrock of justice, equality, and freedom, shaping societies and transforming civilizations. This book, "The Progression of Human Rights: From Magna Carta to Modern Movements," embarks on a journey through time to explore the milestones that have forged the path of human rights as we know them today.

Our story begins in the year 1215 with the Magna Carta, a revolutionary document that planted the seeds of liberty and limited the powers of the monarchy, setting the stage for future generations to demand their inherent rights. From the sparks of the Renaissance that ignited a quest for individual dignity, to the profound philosophies of the Enlightenment that envisioned a world of rationality and equal opportunity, each era contributed to the evolving tapestry of human rights.

The Age of Revolutions marked a turning point, as the American and French revolutions heralded declarations that resonated with cries for liberty and equality. The abolitionist movements that followed shattered the chains of slavery, recognizing the fundamental humanity of every individual. The Industrial Revolution brought new challenges and reforms, as labor rights came to the forefront, demanding fair treatment and safe working conditions for all.

The 20th century was a century of rapid transformation. The suffrage movements fought tirelessly to secure voting rights for women, reshaping political landscapes and empowering half the world's population. In the aftermath of two devastating world wars, the creation of the League of Nations and the Universal Declaration of Human Rights marked a collective commitment to global peace and human dignity.

The decolonization movements of the mid-20th century dismantled empires and championed the self-determination of nations.

The Civil Rights Movement in the United States, and the anti-apartheid struggle in South Africa, demonstrated the power of collective action against systemic injustice. Concurrently, the fight for the rights of children, indigenous peoples, and those with disabilities gained momentum, highlighting the necessity of inclusivity and respect for all.

In recent decades, new frontiers of human rights have emerged. Digital rights advocate for privacy and freedom in an interconnected world, while environmental rights recognize the intrinsic link between a healthy planet and the well-being of its inhabitants. Refugee protections call for compassion and humanity in the face of displacement, and global human rights initiatives seek to uphold justice across borders.

This book is a tribute to the relentless pursuit of human dignity and equality. It is a testament to the countless individuals and movements that have fought against oppression and injustice, paving the way for a more equitable world. As we delve into each chapter, we not only honor the past but also reflect on the ongoing struggles and aspirations that continue to shape our collective future.

Welcome to a journey through history, where each milestone brings us closer to the realization of universal human rights.

# Chapter 1: Magna Carta

The Magna Carta, also known as the Great Charter, is one of the most significant documents in the history of human rights and constitutional law. Sealed by King John of England in 1215, it marked a turning point in the struggle between the monarchy and the feudal barons. The Magna Carta's creation was driven by the dissatisfaction of barons with King John's heavy-handed rule, particularly his excessive taxation and arbitrary justice. The barons, backed by other rebellious elements in society, forced the king to negotiate and eventually agree to a series of demands that were enshrined in the Magna Carta.

The Magna Carta was originally conceived as a practical solution to the political crisis of the time. It sought to limit the powers of the king and ensure certain legal rights for the barons and, to some extent, for all free men in England. One of its most notable aspects is the establishment of the principle that the king was subject to the law, rather than above it. This was revolutionary, as it countered the prevailing notion of the divine right of kings, where monarchs were considered to be accountable only to God.

Among its numerous clauses, the Magna Carta included provisions for the protection of church rights, protection for the barons from illegal imprisonment, access to swift justice, and limitations on feudal payments to the Crown. One of the most famous clauses, Clause 39, states that no free man shall be imprisoned, dispossessed, outlawed, exiled, or in any way harmed except by the lawful judgment of his peers or by the law of the land. This clause laid the foundation for the concept of due process, which would become a cornerstone of legal systems around the world.

Another significant clause was Clause 40, which declared, "To no one will we sell, to no one deny or delay right or justice." This principle underscored the commitment to fair and equitable justice, free from corruption and undue influence, setting a precedent for future legal reforms. Additionally, the Magna Carta addressed economic issues, such as standardizing measures for wine, ale, and corn, and the removal of fish weirs from rivers, which were seen as obstructions to trade and commerce.

While the Magna Carta was initially a peace treaty between King John and the rebellious barons, it quickly became a symbol of broader principles of justice and liberty. Despite its immediate failure to secure lasting peace—King John sought and received annulment of the Magna Carta from Pope Innocent III, leading to continued conflict—it set a precedent that would be invoked repeatedly in the centuries to follow.

The Magna Carta's legacy was revitalized in the 17th century during the conflict between the monarchy and Parliament in England. Key figures, such as Sir Edward Coke, a prominent jurist and Member of Parliament, interpreted and expanded the Magna Carta's principles to argue against the arbitrary powers of the monarchy. Coke's interpretation emphasized the Magna Carta as a timeless safeguard of liberty and due process, influencing legal thought and constitutional development.

The Magna Carta's impact extended beyond England's borders, influencing legal traditions in other parts of the world. Its principles were foundational for the development of common law and were carried to the American colonies, where they profoundly influenced the United States Constitution and the Bill of Rights. The Fifth Amendment to the U.S. Constitution, for instance, echoes the Magna Carta's guarantee of due process, declaring that no person shall be deprived of life, liberty, or property without due process of law.

In contemporary times, the Magna Carta continues to be a potent symbol of the rule of law and the protection of individual rights. It is often cited in legal arguments and political discourse as a foundational document that embodies the principles of justice, fairness, and the limitation of arbitrary power. Celebrations of its anniversaries, particularly the 800th anniversary in 2015, have reinforced its enduring significance in modern legal and political thought.

The Magna Carta's influence can also be seen in international human rights instruments. The Universal Declaration of Human Rights, adopted by the United Nations in 1948, and subsequent human rights treaties, reflect the Magna Carta's legacy in their emphasis on the rule of law, due process, and the protection of individual freedoms.

# Chapter 2: Renaissance Rights

The Renaissance, spanning roughly from the 14th to the 17th century, was a period of profound cultural, artistic, intellectual, and social transformation in Europe. This era is often credited with bridging the gap between the Middle Ages and modern history. One of the most significant yet often overlooked aspects of the Renaissance is its contribution to the development of human rights. The period's emphasis on individualism, humanism, and the questioning of traditional authority laid the groundwork for many of the rights and freedoms we recognize today.

The Renaissance began in Italy and gradually spread across Europe. It was characterized by a renewed interest in the classical art, literature, and philosophies of ancient Greece and Rome. This revival of classical learning had a profound impact on the intellectual life of the time, leading to the development of humanism. Humanism was an intellectual movement that focused on the potential and achievements of individuals. It emphasized the study of subjects such as literature, history, and philosophy, known collectively as the humanities. This shift towards human-centric thinking was revolutionary, as it moved away from the medieval scholasticism that dominated European thought, which was more focused on religious studies and the afterlife.

One of the critical aspects of humanism was its emphasis on the dignity and worth of the individual. Humanist thinkers like Petrarch, Erasmus, and Thomas More believed that individuals had the capacity for reason, creativity, and moral decision-making. This belief in human potential and agency laid the intellectual foundation for the concept of individual rights. By advocating for the education and intellectual development of individuals, humanists argued that people should have the freedom to think, learn, and express themselves.

The invention of the printing press by Johannes Gutenberg around 1440 played a crucial role in the spread of Renaissance ideas. The printing press allowed for the mass production of books, making literature and scholarly works more accessible to a broader audience. This democratization of knowledge contributed to the spread of humanist ideas and the questioning of traditional authorities, including the Church and the monarchy. As more people became literate and educated, they began to demand more personal and political freedoms.

The Renaissance also saw significant developments in political thought that contributed to the evolution of human rights. Niccolò Machiavelli, in his work "The Prince," explored the dynamics of power and governance, arguing that rulers should be pragmatic and shrewd to maintain their power. While Machiavelli's work is often seen as a guide for tyrants, it also contributed to the discourse on political authority and the rights of subjects. Machiavelli's contemporary, Thomas More, offered a contrasting vision in his work "Utopia," which described an ideal society based on equality, shared property, and religious tolerance. More's vision, although fictional, provided a critical perspective on social justice and individual rights.

Another pivotal figure was Jean Bodin, a French political philosopher who wrote during the late Renaissance. Bodin is best known for his theory of sovereignty, which he articulated in "Six Books of the Commonwealth." He argued that absolute sovereignty resided in the state, but he also believed that rulers should respect the fundamental rights of their subjects. Bodin's work laid the groundwork for later theories of social contract and natural rights.

Religious reformations during the Renaissance also had a profound impact on the development of human rights. The Protestant Reformation, initiated by Martin Luther in 1517, challenged the authority of the Catholic Church and emphasized the importance of individual faith and conscience. Luther's assertion that individuals should read and interpret the Bible for themselves encouraged literacy and personal responsibility. This emphasis on individual conscience and the right to religious self-determination contributed to the broader discourse on freedom of thought and expression.

The Reformation also led to significant political and social upheavals, as various regions in Europe grappled with religious conflict and the assertion of national sovereignty. The Peace of Westphalia in 1648, which ended the Thirty Years' War, recognized the principle of cuius regio, eius religio, allowing rulers to determine the religion of their own states. While this principle still placed significant power in the hands of rulers, it also marked a step towards the recognition of religious plurality and the rights of individuals to practice their faith.

In the realm of art and literature, Renaissance figures like Leonardo da Vinci, Michelangelo, and William Shakespeare explored themes of individuality, human emotion, and social justice. Leonardo's notebooks, filled with detailed anatomical drawings and explorations of human proportion, celebrated the complexity and beauty of the human form. Michelangelo's sculptures, such as David, depicted the human body in a way that emphasized its strength and dignity. Shakespeare's plays, with their rich character development and exploration of human nature, highlighted the complexities of individual identity and moral choice.

The Renaissance also saw the emergence of early feminist thought, as women began to challenge their traditional roles in society. Figures like Christine de Pizan, an early feminist writer, advocated for the education and intellectual empowerment of women. In her work "The Book of the City of Ladies," de Pizan argued that women had the same intellectual capabilities as men and should be afforded the same opportunities for education and self-expression. This early advocacy for gender equality was an essential precursor to the later development of women's rights.

The scientific advancements of the Renaissance also contributed to the evolution of human rights. The Scientific Revolution, which began during the Renaissance and continued into the 17th century, fundamentally changed the way people understood the world. Figures like Copernicus, Galileo, and Newton challenged traditional beliefs about the cosmos and the natural world, emphasizing observation, experimentation, and reason. This new approach to knowledge encouraged critical thinking and skepticism towards established authorities, including those in political and religious spheres.

# Chapter 3: Enlightenment Ideas

The Enlightenment, also known as the Age of Reason, was a cultural and intellectual movement that dominated the world of ideas in Europe during the 17th and 18th centuries. It was characterized by an emphasis on reason, science, and individualism rather than tradition and religious authority. The Enlightenment fostered an environment where questioning established norms and seeking knowledge through empirical evidence became the norm. This intellectual revolution played a crucial role in the development of modern political, social, and human rights theories.

The roots of the Enlightenment can be traced back to the Scientific Revolution of the 16th and 17th centuries, which saw significant advances in fields such as astronomy, physics, biology, and chemistry. Scientists like Copernicus, Galileo, and Newton challenged the traditional Aristotelian view of the cosmos and laid the groundwork for a new scientific methodology based on observation, experimentation, and reason. The successes of the Scientific Revolution helped to undermine the authority of the Church and traditional sources of knowledge, paving the way for Enlightenment thinkers to apply the same principles of reason and empiricism to human society and governance.

One of the central ideas of the Enlightenment was the belief in the power of human reason. Enlightenment thinkers, or philosophes, argued that through reason, humans could understand and improve the world. This belief in progress and the perfectibility of human society was a significant departure from the medieval worldview, which often emphasized the fallen nature of humanity and the futility of worldly endeavors. The Enlightenment's faith in reason was also reflected in its rejection of superstition and religious dogma. While not all Enlightenment thinkers were atheists, many were deists, believing in a rational creator who did not intervene in human affairs. This deistic view of God aligned with their emphasis on reason and natural laws.

John Locke, an English philosopher, is often regarded as one of the most influential Enlightenment thinkers. Locke's theories of government and human nature were foundational to the development of modern political thought. In his "Two Treatises of Government," Locke argued that all individuals possess natural rights to life, liberty, and property. He maintained that governments are formed through a social contract to protect these rights, and that any government that fails to do so loses its legitimacy and can be justifiably overthrown. Locke's ideas on natural rights and the social contract were revolutionary, providing a philosophical justification for the Glorious Revolution of 1688 in England and later influencing the American and French Revolutions.

The concept of natural rights was further developed by other Enlightenment thinkers, including Jean-Jacques Rousseau. In his seminal work "The Social Contract," Rousseau argued that true political authority arises from a collective agreement among individuals to form a community governed by the general will. Rousseau believed that individuals, by entering into this social contract, could achieve true freedom, as they would be obeying laws, they had a hand in creating. While Rousseau's ideas differed from Locke's in some respects, particularly regarding the nature of property and the role of direct democracy, both philosophers contributed to the Enlightenment discourse on individual rights and the legitimacy of government.

Voltaire, another prominent Enlightenment thinker, was a fierce advocate for civil liberties, including freedom of speech and religion. Voltaire's wit and sharp criticism of the Church and the French monarchy made him a controversial figure, but his writings were instrumental in spreading Enlightenment ideas. In his numerous letters, essays, and books, Voltaire championed the values of tolerance, reason, and individual freedom. His famous declaration, "I disapprove of what you say, but I will defend to the death your right to say it," encapsulates the Enlightenment commitment to free expression and the protection of individual rights.

The Enlightenment also saw the emergence of economic theories that challenged traditional mercantilist policies. Adam Smith, a Scottish economist, is often regarded as the father of modern economics. In his seminal work "The Wealth of Nations," Smith argued for the benefits of free markets and the division of labor. He introduced the concept of the "invisible hand," suggesting that individuals pursuing their self-interest in a competitive marketplace would unintentionally promote the public good. Smith's ideas laid the foundation for classical economics and influenced subsequent debates on economic policy and the role of government in regulating markets.

The Enlightenment's emphasis on reason and empirical evidence extended to the field of education. Thinkers like Denis Diderot and Jean le Rond d'Alembert worked to compile and disseminate knowledge through projects like the Encyclopédie, a monumental work that sought to catalog and summarize contemporary human knowledge across a wide range of fields. The Encyclopédie was not just a repository of information but also a tool for challenging traditional authority and promoting Enlightenment values. It aimed to educate the public and encourage critical thinking, reflecting the Enlightenment belief in the transformative power of knowledge.

Enlightenment ideas also had a profound impact on the arts and literature. The period saw a flourishing of literature that emphasized reason, individualism, and social critique. Writers like Jonathan Swift, Daniel Defoe, and Mary Wollstonecraft used their works to explore and criticize societal norms, advocate for social reforms, and promote Enlightenment values. Wollstonecraft, in particular, is notable for her pioneering work in advocating for women's rights. Her book "A Vindication of the Rights of Woman" argued that women should have the same educational opportunities as men and should be regarded as rational beings capable of contributing to society.

In addition to its intellectual and cultural contributions, the Enlightenment had significant political ramifications. Enlightenment ideas inspired a wave of revolutions and reforms across Europe and the Americas. The American Revolution was deeply influenced by Enlightenment principles, with the Declaration of Independence drawing heavily on Locke's theories of natural rights and the social contract. Similarly, the French Revolution was fueled by Enlightenment ideals of liberty, equality, and fraternity. The Declaration of the Rights of Man and of the Citizen, adopted during the French Revolution, reflected the Enlightenment's emphasis on individual rights and the legitimacy of government derived from the consent of the governed.

The Enlightenment also played a crucial role in the abolitionist movement. Enlightenment thinkers like Montesquieu and Voltaire criticized the institution of slavery and argued for the inherent dignity and rights of all human beings. These ideas contributed to the growing abolitionist sentiment in Europe and the Americas, leading to the eventual abolition of the transatlantic slave trade and slavery itself in many parts of the world.

Despite its many contributions, the Enlightenment was not without its critics and limitations. Some Enlightenment thinkers, such as Rousseau, were skeptical of the emphasis on reason and progress, warning that it could lead to a neglect of emotions and the complexities of human nature. Additionally, the Enlightenment's focus on European intellectual traditions often marginalized non-European perspectives and cultures. The legacy of the Enlightenment is therefore complex, as it laid the groundwork for modern democratic and human rights principles while also reflecting the biases and limitations of its time.

# Chapter 4: American Revolution

The American Revolution, which took place between 1765 and 1783, was a pivotal event in the history of human rights, marking the birth of the United States of America and setting the stage for the development of democratic ideals and individual liberties. The roots of the revolution lay in the growing discontent among the American colonies over British rule, which was characterized by taxation without representation, restrictions on trade and manufacturing, and the perceived infringement on the rights of the colonists. The ideological foundation of the revolution was deeply influenced by Enlightenment thinkers such as John Locke, whose theories on natural rights and the social contract resonated with the American colonists.

The relationship between the American colonies and the British Crown began to deteriorate following the Seven Years' War (1756-1763). The British government sought to recoup war expenses and tighten control over its American territories through a series of taxes and laws, such as the Stamp Act of 1765, the Townshend Acts of 1767, and the Tea Act of 1773. These measures were met with fierce resistance from the colonists, who argued that they were being taxed without their consent, as they had no representation in the British Parliament. The rallying cry of "no taxation without representation" encapsulated their demand for greater political autonomy and respect for their rights as Englishmen.

The conflict escalated with incidents like the Boston Massacre in 1770, where British soldiers killed five colonists during a confrontation, and the Boston Tea Party in 1773, where American patriots disguised as Mohawk Indians dumped an entire shipment of tea into Boston Harbor as a protest against the Tea Act. These events galvanized public opinion against British rule and set the stage for the convening of the First Continental Congress in 1774, which sought to coordinate a unified response to British policies. The Congress drafted a Declaration of Rights and Grievances, asserting the colonists' entitlement to the same rights as British citizens and calling for a boycott of British goods.

The outbreak of armed conflict came in April 1775 with the Battles of Lexington and Concord, where colonial militias clashed with British troops. These skirmishes marked the beginning of the Revolutionary War, which would last for eight grueling years. In 1776, the Second Continental Congress took a decisive step by adopting the Declaration of Independence, primarily authored by Thomas Jefferson. This seminal document proclaimed the colonies' separation from Britain and articulated the Enlightenment principles of individual rights and self-governance. It famously stated that "all men are created equal" and endowed with "certain unalienable Rights," among them "Life, Liberty, and the pursuit of Happiness."

The war for independence was not only a military struggle but also a battle of ideas. The Patriots, who supported independence, faced off against Loyalists, who remained loyal to the British Crown. The conflict drew in various segments of society, including Native Americans, African Americans, and women, each with their own stakes and perspectives. The Continental Army, led by General George Washington, endured numerous hardships, including lack of supplies, harsh winters, and defeats in battles. However, their resilience and strategic alliances, notably with France, which provided crucial military and financial support, turned the tide in favor of the American cause.

The war culminated in a decisive American victory at the Battle of Yorktown in 1781, where British General Cornwallis surrendered to Washington. This victory effectively ended major hostilities, and the subsequent Treaty of Paris, signed in 1783, formally recognized the independence of the United States. The American Revolution had far-reaching implications beyond the establishment of a new nation. It inspired revolutionary movements worldwide and contributed to the spread of democratic ideals and the notion of human rights.

In the aftermath of the revolution, the newly independent states faced the daunting task of creating a government that embodied the principles for which they had fought. The initial framework, the Articles of Confederation, proved inadequate due to its weak central authority. This led to the Constitutional Convention of 1787, where delegates crafted the United States Constitution, a document that balanced federal and state powers and enshrined the protection of individual rights. The subsequent addition of the Bill of Rights in 1791, comprising the first ten amendments to the Constitution, explicitly guaranteed fundamental freedoms such as freedom of speech, religion, and the press, and protections against arbitrary government actions.

The American Revolution also had significant social implications. It challenged the traditional hierarchies and prompted debates about the nature of equality and liberty. While the revolution advanced the cause of white male property owners, it exposed contradictions in a society that still practiced slavery and limited the rights of women and indigenous peoples. The rhetoric of liberty and equality sparked abolitionist sentiments and laid the groundwork for future movements advocating civil rights and social justice.

# Chapter 5: French Revolution

The French Revolution, which lasted from 1789 to 1799, was a monumental period in world history that radically transformed French society and had profound implications for the global understanding of human rights, citizenship, and governance. The revolution's origins can be traced to a combination of long-standing social inequalities, financial crises, and the influence of Enlightenment ideas that emphasized reason, individual rights, and the questioning of traditional authority.

In the late 18th century, French society was deeply divided into three estates: the First Estate (the clergy), the Second Estate (the nobility), and the Third Estate (the commoners, including the bourgeoisie, urban workers, and peasants). The Third Estate, despite making up the vast majority of the population, was burdened with heavy taxes and had little political power compared to the privileged First and Second Estates. This social stratification fostered widespread resentment and a desire for change.

The financial crisis that precipitated the revolution was partly due to France's involvement in costly wars, including the American Revolutionary War, which exacerbated the national debt. King Louis XVI's government faced bankruptcy, leading to increased taxes and further economic hardship for the Third Estate. In 1789, in an attempt to address the financial crisis, Louis XVI convened the Estates-General, a representative assembly that had not met since 1614. The Third Estate, frustrated with its lack of representation and influence, declared itself the National Assembly and vowed to draft a new constitution for France.

The revolution began in earnest on July 14, 1789, with the storming of the Bastille, a fortress prison in Paris that symbolized the tyranny of the monarchy. This dramatic event galvanized the revolutionaries and led to the widespread uprising known as the Great

Fear, during which peasants attacked and looted the estates of the nobility. The National Assembly responded by abolishing feudal privileges and enacting the Declaration of the Rights of Man and of the Citizen, a groundbreaking document that proclaimed the principles of liberty, equality, and fraternity. It asserted that all men are born free and equal in rights, including the rights to liberty, property, security, and resistance to oppression.

The initial phase of the revolution saw significant reforms aimed at dismantling the old regime. The National Assembly, later renamed the Constituent Assembly, worked to create a constitutional monarchy, reducing the power of the king and establishing a separation of powers. The Civil Constitution of the Clergy in 1790 sought to bring the Catholic Church under state control, leading to a schism between revolutionaries and devout Catholics. However, these reforms did not satisfy everyone, and tensions continued to rise.

By 1791, the revolution had entered a more radical phase. King Louis XVI's attempted escape to Varennes and subsequent capture eroded trust in the monarchy and fueled calls for a republic. The Legislative Assembly, which replaced the Constituent Assembly, faced mounting pressures from radical groups like the Jacobins and the sans-culottes, who advocated for more drastic changes and greater social equality. The outbreak of war with Austria and Prussia in 1792 further destabilized the situation, as foreign powers sought to crush the revolution and restore the monarchy.

The radicalization of the revolution reached its peak with the fall of the monarchy. In August 1792, the Paris Commune, a radical municipal government, led an insurrection that resulted in the arrest of Louis XVI. The National Convention, which succeeded the Legislative Assembly, declared France a republic and abolished the monarchy. In January 1793, Louis XVI was tried and executed by guillotine, followed by the execution of Queen Marie Antoinette later that year.

The revolution then entered its most tumultuous period, known as the Reign of Terror. Led by the Committee of Public Safety, dominated by figures like Maximilien Robespierre, the revolutionary government sought to defend the revolution from internal and external enemies through widespread purges and executions. The Law of Suspects allowed for the arrest of anyone suspected of counter-revolutionary activities, leading to thousands of deaths, including prominent revolutionaries like Georges Danton and Camille Desmoulins. The Reign of Terror instilled fear and suppressed dissent but also alienated many supporters of the revolution.

Despite the chaos, the revolution achieved significant social and political reforms. The National Convention implemented policies aimed at economic equality, such as the Maximum Price Act to control inflation and measures to distribute land to the peasants. The revolutionary government also promoted secularism and education, abolishing religious institutions and promoting state-run schools. Additionally, the French Revolutionary Wars expanded the revolutionary ideals beyond France's borders, as French armies sought to spread the principles of liberty and equality across Europe.

The Reign of Terror ended with the fall of Robespierre in July 1794, an event known as the Thermidorian Reaction. This marked the beginning of the Directory, a more moderate phase of the revolution. The Directory, a five-member executive body, faced numerous challenges, including ongoing wars, economic instability, and political corruption. While it sought to stabilize the country and consolidate the gains of the revolution, it struggled with inefficiency and lack of popular support.

The revolution ultimately concluded with the rise of Napoleon Bonaparte, a charismatic military leader who capitalized on the instability of the Directory. In 1799, Napoleon staged a coup d'état, known as the Coup of 18 Brumaire, and established the Consulate, with himself as First Consul. Although Napoleon's rule marked the end of the revolutionary period, his subsequent actions as Emperor of France continued to spread revolutionary principles through his Napoleonic Code, which influenced legal systems across Europe.

The French Revolution's legacy is profound and multifaceted. It fundamentally altered the social and political landscape of France, dismantling the feudal system and establishing a precedent for modern democratic governance. The revolution's emphasis on universal human rights and the sovereignty of the people inspired subsequent movements for freedom and equality worldwide. It challenged traditional authority and hierarchies, laying the groundwork for the modern concepts of citizenship and individual rights.

Moreover, the revolution had lasting cultural impacts. It promoted secularism, reason, and scientific inquiry, contributing to the rise of modern secular states. The revolutionary period also saw the flourishing of art, literature, and philosophy, as intellectuals and artists engaged with and critiqued the unfolding events. Figures like Jean-Jacques Rousseau and Voltaire, whose ideas influenced the revolution, became emblematic of the Enlightenment's challenge to the status quo.

However, the revolution also had its darker aspects. The Reign of Terror and the violent purges highlighted the dangers of radicalism and the potential for revolutionary ideals to be co-opted by authoritarianism. The social and political upheaval led to significant human suffering, including widespread violence, economic hardship, and displacement.

# Chapter 6: Abolition of Slavery

The abolition of slavery is a monumental chapter in human history, marking the relentless pursuit of freedom and human dignity. This transformative process unfolded over centuries and across continents, deeply impacting the social, economic, and political landscapes of many nations. The journey from widespread acceptance of slavery to its global condemnation and abolition was complex and multifaceted, involving the persistent efforts of enslaved individuals, abolitionists, and reformers, as well as significant legal and political changes.

Slavery has existed in various forms throughout history, from ancient civilizations to the transatlantic slave trade. In ancient societies such as Greece and Rome, slavery was a common practice, often justified by warfare, debt, or punishment. However, the transatlantic slave trade, which began in the 16th century, marked a particularly brutal and extensive period of enslavement. European colonizers forcibly transported millions of Africans to the Americas, where they were subjected to harsh conditions and dehumanizing treatment. This system of chattel slavery treated enslaved people as property, with no rights or freedoms, and was integral to the economic development of European colonies in the New World.

The abolition movement gained momentum in the 18th century, fueled by Enlightenment ideas that emphasized reason, individual rights, and equality. Philosophers such as John Locke and Montesquieu questioned the moral and legal justifications for slavery, arguing for the inherent rights of all human beings. Religious groups, particularly Quakers and other Protestant denominations, also played a crucial role in the early abolitionist movement. They condemned slavery on moral and theological grounds, advocating for the humane treatment and liberation of enslaved individuals.

The abolition movement took root in Britain, where activists like Granville Sharp, Thomas Clarkson, and William Wilberforce led vigorous campaigns against the slave trade. Clarkson's extensive research and collection of evidence on the atrocities of the slave trade, combined with Wilberforce's passionate advocacy in Parliament, gradually swayed public opinion. The efforts of these abolitionists culminated in the passage of the Slave Trade Act of 1807, which outlawed the transatlantic slave trade in the British Empire. However, this was only a partial victory, as slavery itself remained legal in British colonies.

The next significant milestone was the Slavery Abolition Act of 1833, which abolished slavery throughout the British Empire. This act resulted from years of relentless campaigning and the tireless work of abolitionists who exposed the brutal realities of slavery through publications, speeches, and public mobilization. The act provided for the immediate emancipation of children under six, while adults were to be reclassified as "apprentices" and gradually freed over several years. This "apprenticeship" system, however, was heavily criticized for perpetuating exploitation, leading to its abolition in 1838.

In the United States, the abolition of slavery followed a different trajectory. Slavery was deeply entrenched in the Southern economy, particularly in the cultivation of cotton and tobacco. The abolitionist movement in the U.S. gained strength in the early 19th century, driven by a combination of moral, religious, and political motivations. Key figures like Frederick Douglass, a former enslaved person who became a leading voice in the movement, used powerful oratory and writing to advocate for abolition. Harriet Beecher Stowe's novel "Uncle Tom's Cabin" also played a significant role in shaping public opinion against slavery by depicting its brutal realities.

The abolitionist movement in the U.S. was marked by fierce debates and conflicts. Abolitionists like William Lloyd Garrison adopted radical approaches, demanding immediate emancipation and full civil rights for African Americans, while others favored a more gradual approach. The issue of slavery became increasingly contentious, leading to political crises and violence, such as the Nat Turner Rebellion in 1831 and the violent clashes in "Bleeding Kansas" in the 1850s.

The election of Abraham Lincoln in 1860, on an anti-slavery platform, intensified the national conflict, leading to the secession of Southern states and the outbreak of the Civil War in 1861. The war initially focused on preserving the Union, but it soon became a struggle over the future of slavery. In 1863, Lincoln issued the Emancipation Proclamation, declaring the freedom of all enslaved people in Confederate-held territories. While the proclamation did not immediately free all enslaved individuals, it fundamentally shifted the war's purpose and paved the way for the eventual abolition of slavery.

The culmination of these efforts came with the passage of the Thirteenth Amendment to the U.S. Constitution in 1865, which abolished slavery throughout the United States. This landmark amendment marked a decisive victory for the abolitionist movement and ensured that slavery could not be reinstated. However, the struggle for true equality and civil rights for African Americans was far from over, as the post-war period saw the rise of discriminatory laws and practices that sought to maintain racial hierarchy.

Globally, the abolition of slavery unfolded in various ways across different regions. In Latin America, countries like Haiti and Brazil experienced unique paths to abolition. Haiti's successful slave revolt, led by figures such as Toussaint Louverture, culminated in the establishment of the first independent black republic in 1804. Brazil, on the other hand, was one of the last countries to abolish slavery, finally doing so in 1888 through the Lei Áurea (Golden Law) after years of pressure from abolitionist movements and the declining economic viability of slavery.

In Africa, the abolition of slavery was influenced by both internal and external factors. European colonial powers, often driven by economic and humanitarian considerations, imposed anti-slavery laws in their colonies. However, the legacy of slavery and the continued exploitation of labor persisted in various forms, necessitating ongoing efforts to address its repercussions.

The abolition of slavery also intersected with broader movements for human rights and social justice. The fight against slavery highlighted the importance of legal and political advocacy, grassroots mobilization, and the power of moral and ethical arguments in challenging deeply entrenched systems of oppression. The abolitionist movement laid the groundwork for subsequent struggles for civil rights, labor rights, and equality, inspiring generations of activists to continue the pursuit of justice.

Despite the formal abolition of slavery, its legacy remains deeply embedded in many societies. The descendants of enslaved people continue to face systemic discrimination, economic disparities, and social marginalization. The enduring impacts of slavery are evident in issues such as racial profiling, mass incarceration, and socioeconomic inequality. Addressing these legacies requires a comprehensive approach that includes reparative justice, education, and sustained advocacy for equal rights.

In contemporary times, the fight against modern forms of slavery continues. Human trafficking, forced labor, and exploitation persist in various parts of the world, often targeting vulnerable populations such as migrants, women, and children. Organizations and activists work tirelessly to combat these practices, advocating for stronger laws, enforcement mechanisms, and support for victims. The global community's commitment to eradicating all forms of slavery is reflected in international conventions, such as the United Nations' Sustainable Development Goal 8.7, which aims to end modern slavery and human trafficking by 2030.

# Chapter 7: Industrial Reform

Industrial reform refers to the wide array of social, economic, and political changes that emerged in response to the profound transformations brought about by the Industrial Revolution, which began in the late 18th century and continued through the 19th century. The Industrial Revolution, characterized by the shift from agrarian economies to industrialized and urbanized societies, introduced new technologies, production methods, and organizational structures that drastically altered the fabric of everyday life. However, it also brought about significant social challenges, including exploitative labor practices, poor working conditions, child labor, and environmental degradation, necessitating various reform movements aimed at addressing these issues and improving the well-being of workers and communities.

The Industrial Revolution originated in Britain and soon spread to other parts of Europe and North America. Innovations such as the steam engine, mechanized textile production, and advancements in iron and steel manufacturing revolutionized industries and boosted productivity. Factories sprang up, cities expanded rapidly, and new classes of industrial capitalists and wage laborers emerged. While these developments contributed to economic growth and technological progress, they also led to overcrowded cities, inadequate housing, and unsanitary living conditions for the working class. The stark contrast between the wealth of industrialists and the plight of workers sparked demands for reform.

One of the earliest responses to the negative impacts of industrialization was the establishment of labor unions. Workers began organizing to collectively bargain for better wages, shorter working hours, and safer working conditions. The combination of long hours, low pay, and hazardous environments made the need for collective action urgent. The formation of unions faced significant resistance from employers and the government, who often viewed them as threats to economic stability and social order. Despite these obstacles, labor movements gradually gained momentum, with landmark events such as the Peterloo Massacre of 1819 in Manchester, England, where a peaceful rally for parliamentary reform and workers' rights was violently suppressed, highlighting the need for legal protections for workers' rights to organize and protest.

A major milestone in the labor reform movement was the passage of the Factory Acts in Britain. The first of these, the Factory Act of 1833, was a significant step in regulating working conditions, particularly for children. The act limited the working hours for children and required factory owners to provide some education to child workers. Subsequent acts in the mid-19th century expanded these regulations, setting maximum working hours for women and older children and improving safety standards. These legislative efforts, though initially limited in scope and enforcement, laid the groundwork for broader labor protections and reflected growing public awareness and concern about the exploitation of industrial workers.

The push for industrial reform was not limited to labor conditions. The rise of urbanization brought about by industrialization also necessitated reforms in public health and housing. The rapid growth of cities often outpaced the development of adequate infrastructure, leading to overcrowded and unsanitary living conditions that contributed to the spread of diseases such as cholera and tuberculosis. Reformers like Edwin Chadwick in Britain advocated for comprehensive sanitary reforms, emphasizing the importance of clean water, proper sewage systems, and improved housing to promote public health. Chadwick's efforts culminated in the Public Health Act of 1848, which established local boards of health and laid the foundation for modern public health systems.

In addition to addressing labor and public health issues, industrial reform also encompassed educational reforms. The rise of industrial society created a demand for a more educated workforce capable of handling complex machinery and administrative tasks. Reformers argued that education was essential not only for economic productivity but also for social mobility and informed citizenship. The establishment of compulsory education laws in various countries aimed to provide basic education to all children, reducing the reliance on child labor and equipping future generations with the skills needed for a rapidly changing economy.

The impact of industrial reform was further amplified by the work of social reformers and philanthropists who sought to alleviate the harsh realities of industrial life. Figures such as Robert Owen, a factory owner and social reformer, implemented progressive practices in his own enterprises, such as reducing working hours, providing decent housing, and offering education for workers' children. Owen's model communities, such as New Lanark in Scotland, demonstrated that industrial enterprises could be both profitable and humane, influencing broader debates on social responsibility and corporate ethics.

The drive for industrial reform was also influenced by the rise of socialist and communist ideologies, which critiqued the capitalist system and called for radical changes to address the inequalities exacerbated by industrialization. Thinkers like Karl Marx and Friedrich Engels argued that the exploitation of labor was inherent to capitalism and advocated for the abolition of private property and the establishment of a classless society. The spread of socialist ideas inspired labor movements and reformist policies, contributing to the establishment of social safety nets and welfare programs in various countries.

In the United States, industrial reform took on distinct characteristics, shaped by the rapid industrialization and urbanization of the late 19th and early 20th centuries. The Progressive Era, spanning from the 1890s to the 1920s, was marked by a wave of social activism and political reform aimed at addressing the problems caused by industrialization. Progressive reformers targeted issues such as child labor, corruption, corporate monopolies, and workers' rights. The establishment of labor laws, antitrust regulations, and social welfare programs reflected the influence of Progressive ideas on American society.

One of the most significant achievements of the Progressive Era was the introduction of labor legislation that improved working conditions and established protections for workers. The Fair Labor Standards Act of 1938, for instance, set minimum wage standards, regulated working hours, and prohibited oppressive child labor, marking a major victory for the labor movement. These reforms were often the result of intense advocacy and lobbying by labor unions, social reformers, and sympathetic politicians who recognized the need for government intervention to ensure fair and humane treatment of workers.

The global impact of industrial reform extended beyond Europe and North America. In many parts of the world, the experience of industrialization and the struggle for reform were shaped by colonialism and imperialism. Colonized regions often served as sources of raw materials and labor for industrial powers, leading to exploitative labor practices and resistance movements. The fight for labor rights and social justice in these contexts was intertwined with broader struggles for independence and self-determination.

In the 20th century, the rise of international organizations and the adoption of human rights frameworks further advanced the cause of industrial reform. The International Labour Organization (ILO), established in 1919, played a pivotal role in promoting labor standards and advocating for workers' rights globally. The ILO's conventions and recommendations on issues such as working hours, child labor, forced labor, and occupational safety and health provided a basis for national legislation and international cooperation.

The post-World War II period saw the consolidation of welfare states in many industrialized countries, reflecting the influence of industrial reform movements. Governments implemented policies aimed at reducing economic inequality, providing social security, and ensuring access to education, healthcare, and housing. These reforms were often accompanied by strong labor movements that continued to advocate for workers' rights and social justice.

Despite the significant achievements of industrial reform, challenges and disparities remain. The rise of globalization, technological advancements, and shifts in economic structures have introduced new forms of labor exploitation and inequality. Issues such as the gig economy, precarious work, and the erosion of labor protections in certain sectors underscore the ongoing need for vigilance and advocacy in the pursuit of fair and equitable labor practices.

In contemporary times, the legacy of industrial reform continues to inspire movements for social and economic justice. The principles of fair wages, safe working conditions, and the right to organize remain central to labor activism. Additionally, the integration of environmental sustainability into industrial practices reflects a growing recognition of the need to balance economic development with ecological stewardship.

The COVID-19 pandemic has further highlighted the importance of protecting workers' rights and ensuring social safety nets. The pandemic exposed vulnerabilities in labor markets and social systems, prompting renewed calls for robust public health infrastructure, equitable access to healthcare, and comprehensive social protection measures.

# Chapter 8: Women's Suffrage

Women's suffrage, the right of women to vote and run for office, represents one of the most significant achievements in the history of social and political reform. The movement for women's suffrage spanned over a century and involved a broad coalition of activists and reformers who fought against deeply entrenched gender biases and societal norms. The struggle for women's voting rights was characterized by relentless advocacy, strategic mobilization, and, at times, significant personal sacrifices. It culminated in the enfranchisement of women in many countries, marking a monumental shift toward gender equality and the recognition of women's role in the democratic process.

The origins of the women's suffrage movement can be traced back to the late 18th and early 19th centuries, a period marked by the rise of democratic ideals and revolutionary movements. The Enlightenment era, with its emphasis on individual rights and equality, provided an intellectual foundation for the early suffragists. Thinkers like Mary Wollstonecraft, whose seminal work "A Vindication of the Rights of Woman" (1792) argued for the education and empowerment of women, laid the groundwork for subsequent generations of activists.

The formal beginning of the women's suffrage movement is often associated with the Seneca Falls Convention held in 1848 in Seneca Falls, New York. Organized by Elizabeth Cady Stanton and Lucretia Mott, the convention was the first women's rights convention in the United States. It produced the Declaration of Sentiments, a document modeled on the Declaration of Independence, which asserted the equality of men and women and called for women's right to vote. This event marked the start of organized efforts to secure voting rights for women and galvanized support for the cause.

In the United States, the women's suffrage movement gained momentum through the tireless work of activists such as Susan B.

Anthony, Elizabeth Cady Stanton, Sojourner Truth, and later, Carrie Chapman Catt and Alice Paul. These leaders adopted various strategies, from grassroots organizing to lobbying and public demonstrations. The National American Woman Suffrage Association (NAWSA), led by Anthony and Stanton, focused on state-by-state campaigns to secure voting rights, while the more militant National Woman's Party, founded by Alice Paul, employed tactics such as hunger strikes and picketing the White House to draw attention to the cause.

The movement faced substantial opposition from various quarters, including politicians, religious leaders, and even some women who believed that suffrage would disrupt traditional gender roles. Arguments against women's suffrage ranged from concerns about women's supposed lack of political knowledge to fears that it would undermine family structures. Despite these challenges, suffragists persevered, using both peaceful advocacy and civil disobedience to press their demands.

The turning point for women's suffrage in the United States came with the ratification of the 19th Amendment in 1920, which prohibited the denial of the right to vote on the basis of sex. This victory was the result of decades of relentless campaigning and the shifting social and political landscape, including women's significant contributions to the workforce and the war effort during World War I. The passage of the 19th Amendment enfranchised millions of American women, although it did not immediately ensure voting rights for all women, particularly African American women in the South, who continued to face disenfranchisement through discriminatory practices until the civil rights movement of the 1960s.

In parallel to the developments in the United States, the women's suffrage movement gained traction in other parts of the world. In the United Kingdom, the struggle for women's voting rights was marked by the efforts of suffragists and suffragettes. The suffragists, led by figures such as Millicent Fawcett and the National Union of Women's Suffrage

Societies (NUWSS), advocated for suffrage through peaceful means, including lobbying and education. On the other hand, the suffragettes, led by Emmeline Pankhurst and her daughters Christabel and Sylvia through the Women's Social and Political Union (WSPU), adopted more militant tactics, including protests, hunger strikes, and acts of civil disobedience. The outbreak of World War I and women's substantial contributions to the war effort helped shift public opinion, leading to the Representation of the People Act 1918, which granted voting rights to women over the age of 30. Full equal suffrage was achieved a decade later with the Representation of the People (Equal Franchise) Act 1928, which extended the vote to all women over the age of 21.

The push for women's suffrage was not limited to the United States and the United Kingdom. Women in other countries also fought for and won the right to vote, often inspired by the successes of their counterparts abroad. In New Zealand, women achieved suffrage relatively early, with the passage of the Electoral Act in 1893, making New Zealand the first self-governing country to grant women the right to vote. This milestone was largely due to the efforts of suffrage campaigners like Kate Sheppard and the Women's Christian Temperance Union (WCTU).

In Australia, the suffrage movement saw significant progress in the early 20th century. The Commonwealth Franchise Act of 1902 granted voting rights to white women, making Australia the second country to allow women to vote at the national level and the first to allow women to stand for Parliament. However, it is important to note that Indigenous women, along with Indigenous men, were excluded from these rights until much later, reflecting the intersectional nature of suffrage struggles.

In Nordic countries, women's suffrage was achieved relatively early as well. Finland granted women the right to vote and run for office in 1906, becoming the first European country to do so. Norway followed in 1913, Denmark in 1915, and Sweden in 1919. These advances were influenced by broader social reforms and the active involvement of women in public life.

The suffrage movement also made significant strides in other regions, albeit with varying timelines and challenges. In Canada, women gained the right to vote in federal elections in 1918, with some provinces granting suffrage earlier and others later. In Latin America, the women's suffrage movement gained momentum in the early to mid-20th century, with countries like Ecuador (1929), Brazil (1932), and Argentina (1947) enfranchising women. In Asia, women's suffrage movements emerged in the context of broader struggles for independence and social reform. Japan granted women the right to vote in 1945, India in 1950 with the adoption of its new constitution, and China in 1949 following the communist revolution.

The Middle East and North Africa region witnessed more gradual progress in women's suffrage. Turkey granted women the right to vote in 1934 as part of Mustafa Kemal Atatürk's modernization efforts. In other countries, the struggle for suffrage was intertwined with broader social and political transformations. For example, women in Egypt gained the right to vote in 1956, following the revolution that led to the establishment of the republic. In more conservative societies, women's suffrage was achieved later, with Saudi Arabia granting women the right to vote and run in municipal elections only in 2015.

The global movement for women's suffrage was characterized by a diverse array of strategies, coalitions, and influences. While the specifics of the struggle varied from country to country, common themes included the fight against patriarchal structures, the demand for political and social equality, and the mobilization of women from various backgrounds and classes. The movement also faced significant opposition, often rooted in cultural, religious, and political conservatism.

One of the notable aspects of the women's suffrage movement was its intersection with other social justice causes. Many suffragists were also involved in campaigns for abolition, temperance, labor rights, and education reform. The interconnected nature of these movements underscored the broader struggle for human rights and social justice, highlighting the importance of solidarity and collective action.

The impact of women's suffrage extends beyond the right to vote. The enfranchisement of women has had profound implications for societies, contributing to greater gender equality, political participation, and social reforms. Women's presence in the political arena has led to more inclusive policies and legislation addressing issues such as reproductive rights, childcare, education, and gender-based violence. Moreover, the success of the suffrage movement has inspired subsequent generations of activists to continue the fight for gender equality and women's rights in various spheres of life.

Despite the significant progress made, challenges and disparities persist. In many parts of the world, women continue to face barriers to full political participation, including discrimination, violence, and underrepresentation in leadership positions. The ongoing struggle for gender parity in politics and decision-making underscores the need for continued advocacy and reforms to ensure that the gains achieved through the women's suffrage movement are fully realized.

# Chapter 9: League of Nations

The League of Nations represents one of the most significant experiments in international diplomacy and governance in the early 20th century. Conceived in the aftermath of World War I, the League was the first international organization aimed at maintaining world peace and fostering cooperation among nations. Its creation marked a significant departure from the traditional balance-of-power politics that had dominated international relations for centuries. Despite its ultimate failure to prevent the outbreak of World War II, the League of Nations laid the groundwork for modern international institutions, most notably the United Nations.

The origins of the League of Nations can be traced back to the devastation of World War I, which had wrought unprecedented destruction and loss of life. The war exposed the limitations of existing diplomatic practices and the dangers of unchecked militarism and nationalism. As the war drew to a close, there was a widespread recognition among statesmen and intellectuals that a new system was needed to prevent such a catastrophe from recurring. This sentiment was captured by U.S. President Woodrow Wilson, who became a leading advocate for the establishment of a League of Nations.

Wilson's vision for the League was outlined in his famous Fourteen Points speech delivered to the U.S. Congress in January 1918. The Fourteen Points were a set of principles intended to guide the post-war peace negotiations and included the call for the creation of a general association of nations. This association, Wilson argued, would provide a platform for resolving international disputes, promoting disarmament, and ensuring collective security. The idea was to replace the secretive and competitive diplomacy of the past with a transparent and cooperative international order.

The League of Nations was formally established by the Treaty of Versailles in 1919, which ended World War I. The Covenant of the

League of Nations was included as part of the treaty, outlining the structure, goals, and functions of the organization. The Covenant consisted of 26 articles that detailed the mechanisms for maintaining peace and promoting international cooperation. It emphasized the principles of collective security, arbitration, and disarmament, and established procedures for addressing international disputes.

The League's structure comprised three main bodies: the Assembly, the Council, and the Secretariat. The Assembly, which included representatives from all member states, met annually to discuss and vote on matters of international concern. Each member had one vote, and decisions required a two-thirds majority. The Council, a smaller body, consisted of permanent members (initially the United Kingdom, France, Italy, and Japan) and non-permanent members elected by the Assembly. The Council was responsible for addressing urgent threats to peace and could convene more frequently than the Assembly. The Secretariat, led by the Secretary-General, handled the administrative and operational functions of the League.

One of the League's earliest and most significant achievements was the resolution of the Åland Islands dispute between Sweden and Finland in 1921. The islands, located in the Baltic Sea, were predominantly Swedish-speaking but had been under Finnish control since the early 19th century. The inhabitants sought to reunite with Sweden, leading to tensions between the two countries. The League intervened by conducting a thorough investigation and ultimately recommended that the islands remain under Finnish sovereignty but with guarantees for the cultural and linguistic rights of the Swedish-speaking population. Both Sweden and Finland accepted the League's decision, demonstrating the potential for peaceful conflict resolution through international mediation.

The League also played a role in addressing the humanitarian crisis following World War I, particularly the plight of refugees and prisoners of war. Under the leadership of Fridtjof Nansen, the League's High

Commissioner for Refugees, efforts were made to repatriate and resettle millions of displaced individuals. Nansen developed the Nansen passport, a travel document for stateless refugees, which facilitated their movement and resettlement. These initiatives marked an early attempt at international cooperation in managing refugee crises, setting precedents for future humanitarian efforts.

Despite these successes, the League of Nations faced numerous challenges and limitations. One of the most significant issues was the absence of the United States, which never joined the League despite President Wilson's pivotal role in its creation. The U.S. Senate, led by isolationist and nationalist factions, rejected the Treaty of Versailles and, by extension, the League of Nations Covenant. The absence of the world's most powerful nation undermined the League's credibility and effectiveness from the outset.

Additionally, the League's commitment to collective security was repeatedly tested and found wanting. In the 1930s, a series of aggressive actions by authoritarian regimes highlighted the League's inability to enforce its resolutions and prevent conflict. The Japanese invasion of Manchuria in 1931, the Italian invasion of Ethiopia in 1935, and the German remilitarization of the Rhineland in 1936 were all clear violations of international agreements. In each case, the League condemned the actions but lacked the means to enforce its decisions, largely due to the unwillingness of major powers to commit military resources or economic sanctions.

The League's failure to prevent the outbreak of World War II was perhaps its most glaring shortcoming. The rise of totalitarian regimes in Germany, Italy, and Japan, combined with the policy of appeasement adopted by Britain and France, led to a series of unchecked aggressions that culminated in the global conflict of 1939-1945. The League's inability to maintain peace highlighted the need for a more robust and effective system of international governance.

Despite its failures, the League of Nations left a lasting legacy that influenced the development of the post-World War II international order. The principles and structures of the League provided a foundation for the United Nations, which was established in 1945 with the aim of preventing future conflicts and promoting international cooperation. Many of the League's agencies and functions were incorporated into the UN, including the International Labour Organization (ILO) and the mandate system for administering former colonial territories.

The UN built upon the lessons learned from the League's shortcomings, introducing several key changes to enhance its effectiveness. The UN Charter established a stronger framework for collective security, with the Security Council granted the authority to take enforcement action, including the use of military force, to maintain or restore international peace and security. The inclusion of the United States, the Soviet Union, and other major powers as permanent members of the Security Council aimed to ensure the participation of the world's most influential nations in the new international order.

The League of Nations also contributed to the development of international law and norms. Its efforts to promote disarmament, human rights, and social welfare laid the groundwork for subsequent treaties and conventions. The League's experience highlighted the importance of multilateral diplomacy and the need for a comprehensive approach to addressing global challenges.

# Chapter 10: Universal Declaration

The Universal Declaration of Human Rights (UDHR) stands as a monumental document in the history of human rights, symbolizing a collective commitment by the international community to uphold and protect the inherent dignity and equal rights of all members of the human family. Adopted by the United Nations General Assembly on December 10, 1948, the UDHR was a direct response to the atrocities of World War II and the Holocaust, reflecting a universal consensus on the need to ensure that such violations of human rights would never occur again. The declaration's influence extends far beyond its initial adoption, serving as a foundation for international human rights law, inspiring numerous national constitutions and legal frameworks, and guiding the work of countless human rights organizations worldwide.

The drafting of the UDHR was a comprehensive and collaborative effort involving representatives from diverse legal, cultural, and religious backgrounds. This process was chaired by Eleanor Roosevelt, the widow of U.S. President Franklin D. Roosevelt and a prominent advocate for human rights. Other key figures included René Cassin of France, who later won the Nobel Peace Prize for his work on the UDHR; Charles Malik of Lebanon, who brought a philosophical perspective to the discussions; Peng Chun Chang of China, who emphasized the importance of Eastern philosophies and traditions; and John Humphrey of Canada, who prepared the original draft of the declaration. Their combined efforts ensured that the document reflected a wide array of cultural perspectives and philosophical traditions, thus reinforcing its universal applicability.

The UDHR consists of a preamble and 30 articles, each articulating a specific right or set of rights to which all individuals are entitled. The preamble sets the tone by recognizing the inherent dignity and equal and inalienable rights of all members of the human family as the foundation of freedom, justice, and peace in the world. It emphasizes that disregard and contempt for human rights have resulted in barbarous acts that have outraged the conscience of humanity, and that the advent of a world in which human beings shall enjoy freedom of speech and belief and freedom from fear and want has been proclaimed as the highest aspiration of the common people.

Article 1 of the UDHR states that all human beings are born free and equal in dignity and rights. They are endowed with reason and conscience and should act towards one another in a spirit of brotherhood. This foundational principle underscores the universality of human rights and the inherent equality of all people, regardless of their background or circumstances.

Articles 2 through 21 outline a broad spectrum of civil and political rights. These include the right to life, liberty, and security of person (Article 3); freedom from slavery and servitude (Article 4); freedom from torture and cruel, inhuman, or degrading treatment or punishment (Article 5); and the right to recognition as a person before the law (Article 6). The declaration also asserts the right to an effective remedy by competent national tribunals for acts violating fundamental rights (Article 8), the right to a fair and public hearing by an independent and impartial tribunal (Article 10), and the right to be presumed innocent until proven guilty (Article 11).

Additionally, the UDHR addresses issues of privacy, family, and nationality. Article 12 protects individuals from arbitrary interference with their privacy, family, home, or correspondence, and from attacks upon their honor and reputation. Article 13 grants everyone the right to freedom of movement and residence within the borders of each state, as well as the right to leave any country and to return to their own country. Article 15 affirms the right to a nationality and the protection against arbitrary deprivation of nationality or denial of the right to change nationality.

Articles 22 through 27 focus on economic, social, and cultural rights. These include the right to social security (Article 22), the right to work and to just and favorable conditions of work (Article 23), the right to rest and leisure (Article 24), and the right to a standard of living adequate for the health and well-being of oneself and one's family, including food, clothing, housing, and medical care (Article 25). Article 26 emphasizes the right to education, stating that education shall be free, at least in the elementary and fundamental stages, and that higher education shall be equally accessible to all based on merit. Article 27 affirms the right to freely participate in the cultural life of the community, to enjoy the arts, and to share in scientific advancement and its benefits.

The final articles, 28 through 30, address the duties of individuals to their community and the limitations of these rights. Article 28 declares that everyone is entitled to a social and international order in which the rights and freedoms set forth in the declaration can be fully realized. Article 29 recognizes that individuals have duties to the community, and that the exercise of their rights and freedoms may be subject to limitations determined by law, solely for the purpose of securing due recognition and respect for the rights and freedoms of others and of meeting the just requirements of morality, public order, and the general welfare in a democratic society. Article 30 clarifies that nothing in the declaration may be interpreted as implying for any state, group, or person any right to engage in any activity or to perform any act aimed at the destruction of any of the rights and freedoms set forth herein.

The adoption of the UDHR was a landmark event, but its implementation and impact have been varied. While the declaration itself is not legally binding, it has profoundly influenced the development of international human rights law. The principles enshrined in the UDHR have been incorporated into subsequent international treaties, such as the International Covenant on Civil and Political Rights (ICCPR) and the International Covenant on Economic, Social and Cultural Rights (ICESCR), both of which form part of the International Bill of Human Rights alongside the UDHR. These covenants, adopted in 1966 and entering into force in 1976, create binding legal obligations for the states that ratify them, thereby transforming many of the UDHR's principles into enforceable international law.

The UDHR has also inspired numerous regional human rights instruments, including the European Convention on Human Rights (ECHR), the American Convention on Human Rights (ACHR), and the African Charter on Human and Peoples' Rights (ACHPR). These instruments establish regional human rights courts and commissions, providing mechanisms for individuals to seek redress for violations of their rights.

At the national level, the UDHR has influenced the drafting and interpretation of constitutions and legal frameworks around the world. Many countries have incorporated its principles into their domestic laws, thereby strengthening the legal protections for human rights within their jurisdictions. For example, the South African Constitution, adopted in 1996, includes a comprehensive Bill of Rights that reflects many of the principles outlined in the UDHR.

The UDHR has also played a crucial role in the work of human rights organizations and activists. It serves as a benchmark for evaluating the human rights practices of governments and as a tool for advocacy and education. Organizations such as Amnesty International, Human Rights Watch, and the International Federation for Human Rights (FIDH) rely on the UDHR to promote human rights awareness and to hold governments accountable for their obligations.

Despite these achievements, the full realization of the rights enshrined in the UDHR remains an ongoing challenge. Human rights violations continue to occur in many parts of the world, often with impunity. Issues such as discrimination, poverty, conflict, and authoritarianism pose significant obstacles to the protection and promotion of human rights. The gap between the ideals of the UDHR and the reality on the ground highlights the need for continued vigilance, advocacy, and international cooperation.

The impact of the UDHR has also been the subject of debate and critique. Some argue that the declaration reflects Western values and imposes them on diverse cultural and social contexts. Others contend that the universality of human rights must be understood in a way that respects cultural diversity while upholding fundamental principles of dignity and equality. These debates underscore the complex interplay between universal human rights norms and local traditions and practices.

In recent years, new challenges have emerged that test the resilience and relevance of the UDHR. The rise of digital technologies, for example, has introduced new dimensions to human rights, such as the right to privacy in the digital age, freedom of expression online, and the impact of artificial intelligence on employment and social equality. Climate change and environmental degradation have also prompted calls to recognize the right to a healthy environment as a fundamental human right. These issues require innovative approaches and adaptations of existing human rights frameworks to address the evolving landscape of human rights concerns.

Moreover, the COVID-19 pandemic has highlighted and exacerbated existing inequalities, raising critical questions about the right to health, the equitable distribution of vaccines, and the balance between public health measures and individual freedoms. The pandemic has underscored the interconnectedness of human rights, demonstrating that the protection of one right often depends on the protection of others.

# Chapter 11: Decolonization

Decolonization refers to the process by which colonies gained their independence from colonial powers and became sovereign nations. This sweeping movement, which predominantly occurred during the mid-20th century, dramatically reshaped the global political landscape. The phenomenon of decolonization was driven by a combination of factors, including the erosion of European colonial powers' control, rising nationalist movements within colonies, global ideological shifts following World War II, and the influence of international organizations such as the United Nations.

The roots of decolonization can be traced back to the late 19th and early 20th centuries when ideas about self-determination and national sovereignty began to gain traction. The concept that nations have the right to govern themselves was propagated by intellectuals and political leaders worldwide, challenging the legitimacy of imperial rule. However, it was the aftermath of World War II that accelerated the decolonization process. The war had weakened many European powers, both economically and militarily, and exposed the moral contradictions of colonialism, especially given the rhetoric of freedom and democracy that had been used to justify the fight against Axis powers.

One of the earliest significant examples of decolonization was India's independence from British rule in 1947. The Indian independence movement, led by figures such as Mahatma Gandhi and Jawaharlal Nehru, utilized non-violent resistance and civil disobedience to challenge British authority. The Quit India Movement, launched in 1942, marked a critical point in this struggle, demanding an end to British rule. Following a period of intense political negotiation and civil unrest, Britain agreed to partition the subcontinent into two independent states: India and Pakistan. This partition, while granting independence, also led to massive displacement and communal violence, illustrating the complex and often painful process of decolonization.

Following India's independence, a wave of decolonization swept across Asia, Africa, the Middle East, and the Caribbean. In Southeast Asia, Indonesia declared its independence from Dutch colonial rule in 1945, although it was only recognized by the Netherlands in 1949 after a protracted and bloody struggle. Similarly, Vietnam declared its independence from French colonial rule in 1945, leading to the First Indochina War, which resulted in the Geneva Accords of 1954 and the temporary division of Vietnam into North and South.

In Africa, the decolonization process varied significantly from country to country, reflecting the diverse colonial histories and local conditions. Ghana became the first sub-Saharan African country to gain independence in 1957 under the leadership of Kwame Nkrumah, a prominent advocate for Pan-Africanism and anti-colonialism. Ghana's independence served as an inspiration and model for other African nations. In 1960, often referred to as the "Year of Africa," seventeen African countries declared their independence, marking a pivotal moment in the decolonization movement. Among them was Nigeria, Africa's most populous country, which gained independence from Britain on October 1, 1960.

The decolonization of Algeria from French rule is another notable example, characterized by a protracted and violent struggle. The Algerian War of Independence (1954-1962) involved guerrilla warfare, terrorism, and a heavy-handed military response from France. The conflict had a profound impact on French politics and society and culminated in the Evian Accords of 1962, which granted Algeria independence. The war also influenced other anti-colonial movements by highlighting the willingness of colonized people to engage in sustained armed struggle to achieve their freedom.

In the Middle East, decolonization was often intertwined with the complex geopolitics of the Cold War and the creation of new states from former Ottoman territories. The establishment of Israel in 1948, following the end of the British mandate in Palestine, led to ongoing conflict and displacement that continue to affect the region. Egypt gained nominal independence from Britain in 1922, but British influence persisted until the revolution of 1952, which led to the rise of Gamal Abdel Nasser and the subsequent nationalization of the Suez Canal, further solidifying Egypt's sovereignty.

The Caribbean also witnessed significant decolonization movements, often characterized by relatively peaceful transitions to independence. Jamaica and Trinidad and Tobago, for example, both gained independence from Britain in 1962. In many instances, these transitions were facilitated through constitutional negotiations and the establishment of democratic institutions, reflecting a different pattern compared to the often-violent struggles seen in other regions.

The role of international organizations, particularly the United Nations, was crucial in the decolonization process. The UN Charter, established in 1945, included provisions for the promotion of self-determination and the end of colonial rule. The establishment of the UN Special Committee on Decolonization in 1961 provided a forum for colonies to voice their aspirations and for member states to advocate for the end of colonialism. The committee's work, combined with resolutions such as the 1960 Declaration on the Granting of Independence to Colonial Countries and Peoples, underscored the international community's support for decolonization and exerted pressure on colonial powers to relinquish control.

Decolonization also had significant economic, social, and cultural dimensions. Economically, the transition from colonial rule often posed substantial challenges for newly independent states, which had to contend with the legacies of colonial exploitation, underdeveloped infrastructure, and dependency on former colonial powers. Many new nations faced difficulties in establishing sustainable economic growth and diversifying their economies. Efforts to address these challenges led to various development strategies, including state-led industrialization, agrarian reform, and attempts to establish regional economic cooperation.

Socially, decolonization involved the reconstruction of national identities and the reclamation of cultural heritage. Colonialism had often imposed foreign languages, education systems, and cultural practices, leading to the marginalization of indigenous traditions and identities. Post-independence, many countries sought to revive and promote their cultural heritage, languages, and traditions as part of a broader effort to assert their sovereignty and national identity. This process of cultural reclamation was often seen as a vital aspect of decolonization, helping to heal the psychological scars of colonial rule and fostering a sense of pride and unity among the population.

Politically, decolonization often required the establishment of new governance structures and institutions. Many newly independent countries adopted constitutions that emphasized democratic principles, human rights, and social justice. However, the political landscape in these nations was frequently turbulent, with internal conflicts, coups, and authoritarian regimes emerging in the post-independence period. The challenges of nation-building, combined with external pressures from Cold War superpowers, led to varied political trajectories, with some countries achieving stable democracies while others experienced prolonged instability and conflict.

Decolonization also had profound implications for international relations. The emergence of numerous new states in the global arena significantly altered the composition and dynamics of international organizations, particularly the United Nations. The influx of newly independent countries, many of which formed the Non-Aligned Movement, shifted the balance of power and introduced new perspectives and priorities into global discussions. These countries advocated for greater equity in international relations, economic development, and the end of all forms of imperialism and neocolonialism.

The legacy of decolonization continues to shape contemporary global politics and society. The former colonial powers and their erstwhile colonies have had to navigate complex relationships, often characterized by economic dependency, cultural exchange, and political cooperation. The impact of colonialism and the struggle for independence remain deeply embedded in the national consciousness of many countries, influencing their domestic and foreign policies.

Furthermore, the process of decolonization has inspired ongoing movements for self-determination and autonomy among various groups and regions around the world. Indigenous peoples, in particular, have drawn on the principles of decolonization to advocate for their rights, cultural preservation, and political sovereignty. The decolonization experience also serves as a reference point for contemporary struggles against various forms of oppression and exploitation, highlighting the enduring relevance of the principles of justice, equality, and self-determination.

# Chapter 12: Civil Rights Movement

The Civil Rights Movement in the United States was a decades-long struggle to end racial segregation and discrimination against African Americans and to secure legal recognition and federal protection of the citizenship rights enumerated in the Constitution and federal law. This movement spanned from the 1950s through the 1960s, and its roots extended deep into American history, drawing upon earlier efforts for racial equality and justice. The movement employed a variety of tactics, including legal challenges, nonviolent protests, civil disobedience, and grassroots organizing, which collectively dismantled institutionalized racial segregation and transformed American society.

The origins of the Civil Rights Movement can be traced back to the Reconstruction era following the Civil War, when the 13th, 14th, and 15th Amendments were adopted to abolish slavery, grant citizenship to all born in the United States, and protect voting rights regardless of race. However, the end of Reconstruction in 1877 marked the beginning of the Jim Crow era, a period characterized by state and local laws enforcing racial segregation in the Southern United States. African Americans were subjected to systemic discrimination, disenfranchisement, and violence, leading to widespread social and economic inequalities.

One of the earliest significant legal challenges to segregation was the landmark 1896 Supreme Court case Plessy v. Ferguson, which upheld the constitutionality of racial segregation under the doctrine of "separate but equal." This decision provided legal justification for segregation and discrimination, which persisted for decades. However, the groundwork for the modern Civil Rights Movement was laid in the early 20th century through the efforts of organizations such as the National Association for the Advancement of Colored People (NAACP), founded in 1909. The NAACP played a crucial role in challenging segregation and discrimination through litigation and advocacy.

The modern Civil Rights Movement gained momentum in the 1950s, marked by a series of pivotal events and legal victories. One of the most significant milestones was the Supreme Court's decision in Brown v. Board of Education of Topeka in 1954. This landmark case, argued by NAACP attorney Thurgood Marshall, overturned Plessy v. Ferguson by declaring that state laws establishing separate public schools for black and white students were unconstitutional. The Court's unanimous decision stated that "separate educational facilities are inherently unequal," and mandated the desegregation of public schools across America. The Brown decision galvanized the movement and provided a legal basis for challenging segregation in other areas of public life.

The Civil Rights Movement's strategies and tactics were multifaceted, incorporating nonviolent resistance, civil disobedience, and mass mobilization. One of the earliest and most iconic acts of defiance against segregation occurred in Montgomery, Alabama, in 1955, when Rosa Parks, an African American seamstress and NAACP activist, refused to give up her seat to a white passenger on a segregated bus. Her arrest sparked the Montgomery Bus Boycott, a 381-day mass protest led by a young Baptist minister named Martin Luther King Jr. The boycott, which saw African Americans in Montgomery refusing to use the city's buses, resulted in a Supreme Court ruling that declared bus segregation unconstitutional. This victory propelled King into national prominence and established nonviolent protest as a central tactic of the movement.

The Southern Christian Leadership Conference (SCLC), founded in 1957 with King as its first president, became a leading organization in the movement, advocating for nonviolent resistance and civil disobedience. The SCLC coordinated with other civil rights organizations and played a crucial role in organizing protests, marches, and voter registration drives throughout the South.

Another significant organization was the Student Nonviolent Coordinating Committee (SNCC), founded in 1960 by young activists who were inspired by the Greensboro sit-ins. These sit-ins began when four African American college students in Greensboro, North Carolina, sat at a segregated Woolworth's lunch counter and refused to leave until they were served. This act of civil disobedience sparked similar sit-ins across the country and highlighted the power of student activism. SNCC emphasized grassroots organizing and direct action, focusing on voter registration and community empowerment in rural Southern communities.

The Freedom Rides of 1961 were another crucial episode in the Civil Rights Movement, organized by the Congress of Racial Equality (CORE) and SNCC. Integrated groups of activists rode interstate buses into the segregated South to challenge the non-enforcement of Supreme Court rulings that declared segregated public buses unconstitutional. The Freedom Riders faced violent attacks and arrests, drawing national attention to the pervasive racism and brutality in the South. The federal government's intervention to protect the riders underscored the growing pressure on the government to address civil rights issues.

The movement reached a critical juncture with the March on Washington for Jobs and Freedom on August 28, 1963. Organized by a coalition of civil rights, labor, and religious organizations, the march attracted over 250,000 participants who gathered at the Lincoln Memorial to demand civil and economic rights for African Americans. It was here that Martin Luther King Jr. delivered his iconic "I Have a Dream" speech, envisioning a future where people would be judged by the content of their character rather than the color of their skin. The march and King's speech played a pivotal role in galvanizing public support for civil rights legislation.

One of the most significant legislative achievements of the Civil Rights Movement was the Civil Rights Act of 1964. Signed into law by President Lyndon B. Johnson, the Act prohibited discrimination based on race, color, religion, sex, or national origin and ended segregation in public places and banned employment discrimination. The Act also established the Equal Employment Opportunity Commission (EEOC) to enforce federal laws prohibiting workplace discrimination. The passage of the Civil Rights Act was a landmark victory for the movement, but the struggle for voting rights continued.

The struggle for voting rights culminated in the Selma to Montgomery marches in 1965. Organized by SCLC and SNCC, these marches aimed to highlight the barriers to African American voter registration in Alabama. The first march, known as "Bloody Sunday," took place on March 7, 1965, when state troopers and local police brutally attacked peaceful demonstrators as they attempted to cross the Edmund Pettus Bridge in Selma. The violent crackdown was broadcast on national television, shocking the conscience of the nation and leading to widespread outrage. In response, President Johnson addressed a joint session of Congress, urging the passage of the Voting Rights Act. The Selma marches underscored the need for federal intervention to protect voting rights and led to the Voting Rights Act of 1965, which banned discriminatory voting practices and authorized federal oversight of voter registration in areas with a history of discrimination.

The Civil Rights Movement also addressed issues of economic justice and poverty. The Poor People's Campaign, launched by Martin Luther King Jr. and the SCLC in 1968, sought to address economic inequalities and demand economic justice for all Americans. The campaign called for a broad coalition of poor people across racial and ethnic lines to advocate for better housing, employment opportunities, and a living wage. Although King was assassinated in April 1968, the campaign continued under the leadership of Ralph Abernathy, culminating in a march on Washington and the establishment of Resurrection City, a temporary encampment on the National Mall to draw attention to poverty.

The legacy of the Civil Rights Movement is profound and far-reaching. It led to significant legal and social changes, including the dismantling of Jim Crow laws, the desegregation of public schools and facilities, and the protection of voting rights for African Americans. The movement also inspired other marginalized groups, including women, Native Americans, LGBTQ+ individuals, and people with disabilities, to advocate for their rights and seek equality.

The movement's emphasis on nonviolent protest and civil disobedience continues to influence contemporary social justice movements. The principles of nonviolence and grassroots organizing have been adopted by various movements worldwide, including the struggle against apartheid in South Africa, the pro-democracy movements in Eastern Europe, and the fight for civil rights in Northern Ireland.

Despite these achievements, the goals of the Civil Rights Movement remain unfinished. Racial disparities persist in various aspects of American life, including education, employment, housing, and the criminal justice system. The rise of the Black Lives Matter movement in the 21st century highlights the ongoing struggle against systemic racism and police brutality. This movement, which gained international attention following the killing of Trayvon Martin in 2012 and the deaths of Michael Brown, Eric Garner, Breonna Taylor, George Floyd, and others, draws on the legacy of the Civil Rights Movement to demand justice and accountability.

# Chapter 13: Anti-Apartheid Struggle

The anti-apartheid struggle represents one of the most significant movements for human rights in the 20th century, symbolizing the fight against racial discrimination and injustice in South Africa. Apartheid, an Afrikaans word meaning "apartness," was a system of institutionalized racial segregation and discrimination that existed in South Africa from 1948 until the early 1990s. The roots of apartheid can be traced back to colonial history, but it was formally implemented by the National Party government after their election victory in 1948. The policies of apartheid were designed to maintain white supremacy and control over the country's political, economic, and social systems.

The struggle against apartheid began long before 1948, as indigenous African communities and people of mixed race, Indian, and other descent had resisted colonial domination and segregationist practices for centuries. However, the formal anti-apartheid movement gained momentum in the mid-20th century with the formation of several key organizations and the involvement of influential leaders.

One of the most prominent organizations in the anti-apartheid struggle was the African National Congress (ANC), founded in 1912. The ANC initially sought to engage in peaceful dialogue and petition the government for rights and equality. However, as apartheid policies became more entrenched and repressive, the ANC's tactics evolved. Under the leadership of figures like Nelson Mandela, Oliver Tambo, and Walter Sisulu, the ANC adopted more direct forms of resistance, including protests, strikes, and acts of civil disobedience.

A pivotal moment in the anti-apartheid struggle was the Defiance Campaign of 1952. This campaign was a coordinated effort by the ANC and other allied organizations, such as the South African Indian Congress (SAIC), to protest against unjust laws through acts of civil disobedience. Thousands of volunteers deliberately broke apartheid laws, such as curfew regulations and pass laws, which required black

South Africans to carry identification documents at all times. The campaign drew international attention to the oppressive nature of apartheid and mobilized mass participation within South Africa.

The apartheid regime responded to the growing resistance with increasing brutality. The Sharpeville Massacre in 1960 marked a turning point in the struggle. On March 21, 1960, police opened fire on a peaceful protest organized by the Pan Africanist Congress (PAC) against pass laws in the township of Sharpeville, killing 69 people and wounding hundreds. The massacre shocked the world and led to widespread condemnation of the South African government. In the aftermath, the government declared a state of emergency, banned the ANC and PAC, and arrested thousands of activists.

In response to the state's repression, the ANC established an armed wing, Umkhonto we Sizwe ("Spear of the Nation"), in 1961. Led by Nelson Mandela, this group engaged in acts of sabotage against government installations, marking a shift from non-violent protest to armed resistance. Mandela and other leaders were eventually arrested and sentenced to life imprisonment in the Rivonia Trial of 1963-1964, which intended to dismantle the ANC's leadership and quell the movement.

Despite these setbacks, the anti-apartheid struggle continued, both within South Africa and internationally. The global anti-apartheid movement played a crucial role in exerting pressure on the South African government. Activists around the world organized boycotts, protests, and campaigns to isolate the apartheid regime economically and politically. One of the most effective strategies was the call for economic sanctions and disinvestment from South Africa. Countries and companies were urged to sever economic ties with South Africa, and this movement gained significant traction in the 1980s.

Cultural and sporting boycotts also played a critical role in isolating the apartheid regime. South Africa was banned from international sporting events, such as the Olympics and FIFA World

Cup, which highlighted the global opposition to apartheid. Artists, musicians, and performers also refused to visit or perform in South Africa, further raising awareness about the injustices of apartheid.

The internal resistance within South Africa intensified during the 1970s and 1980s. The 1976 Soweto Uprising was a key moment in the struggle. On June 16, 1976, thousands of black schoolchildren in the Soweto township protested against the mandatory use of Afrikaans in schools, which they saw as a symbol of oppression. The police responded with violence, killing hundreds of students. The uprising sparked widespread protests and resistance across the country, leading to a new generation of activists joining the anti-apartheid movement.

During the 1980s, the United Democratic Front (UDF) emerged as a powerful coalition of anti-apartheid organizations. The UDF coordinated various forms of resistance, including boycotts, strikes, and demonstrations. The labor movement, particularly the Congress of South African Trade Unions (COSATU), also played a significant role in challenging the apartheid regime through industrial action and mass mobilization.

International pressure continued to mount on the South African government. In 1986, the United States Congress passed the Comprehensive Anti-Apartheid Act, which imposed economic sanctions on South Africa. Many other countries and multinational corporations followed suit, leading to significant economic challenges for the apartheid regime.

By the late 1980s, it became clear that apartheid was untenable. The South African economy was suffering, and the country faced increasing internal unrest and international isolation. In 1989, F.W. de Klerk became the president of South Africa and began to recognize the need for change. In a historic move, de Klerk announced the unbanning of the ANC and other anti-apartheid organizations in 1990, and he released Nelson Mandela from prison after 27 years of incarceration.

The early 1990s marked a period of intense negotiations and transitional politics in South Africa. The Convention for a Democratic South Africa (CODESA) was established to facilitate discussions between the apartheid government and anti-apartheid groups. These negotiations were fraught with tension and violence, but they ultimately led to the dismantling of apartheid.

In 1994, South Africa held its first democratic elections, open to citizens of all races. Nelson Mandela, representing the ANC, was elected as the first black president of South Africa. The election marked the official end of apartheid and the beginning of a new era for the country.

The anti-apartheid struggle is a testament to the power of collective action, resilience, and the pursuit of justice. It involved sacrifices, immense courage, and unwavering commitment from countless individuals and organizations. The movement not only succeeded in dismantling a brutal system of racial discrimination but also inspired human rights struggles worldwide. The legacy of the anti-apartheid struggle continues to influence global discourses on human rights, equality, and social justice, reminding us of the enduring importance of standing against oppression in all its forms.

# Chapter 14: Child Rights

Child rights refer to the fundamental freedoms and entitlements of children, recognizing them as individuals with their own distinct needs and rights. The evolution of child rights has been a complex and multifaceted journey, shaped by cultural, social, legal, and political developments over centuries. It reflects the growing recognition of children as bearers of rights, deserving of special protection and care due to their vulnerability and developmental needs. This comprehensive exploration of child rights will delve into historical contexts, key milestones, international legal frameworks, and contemporary challenges, highlighting the ongoing efforts to safeguard and promote the rights of children globally.

Historically, children were often seen as property or as economic assets to their families, with limited or no recognition of their individual rights. In many societies, children were expected to work from a young age, often in harsh and hazardous conditions. The Industrial Revolution in the 18th and 19th centuries exacerbated these issues, as child labor became widespread in factories, mines, and other industrial settings. Children worked long hours for minimal wages, often at the expense of their health, education, and overall well-being.

The early efforts to protect children from exploitation and abuse began in the 19th century. Social reformers and philanthropists in Europe and North America campaigned against child labor and advocated for compulsory education. One of the significant milestones during this period was the Factory Act of 1833 in the United Kingdom, which set limits on the working hours of children and required factory owners to provide basic education. Similar legislative measures followed in other countries, gradually improving the conditions for working children and recognizing their right to education.

The early 20th century saw the establishment of organizations dedicated to child welfare and rights. The Save the Children Fund, founded in 1919 by Eglantyne Jebb and her sister Dorothy Buxton in the aftermath of World War I, aimed to provide relief to children affected by war and poverty. Eglantyne Jebb's efforts culminated in the drafting of the Declaration of the Rights of the Child, which was adopted by the League of Nations in 1924. This declaration, also known as the Geneva Declaration, was one of the first international documents to recognize the specific rights of children, emphasizing their need for special protection and care.

The atrocities of World War II and the Holocaust further highlighted the vulnerability of children in times of conflict and crisis. The establishment of the United Nations in 1945 marked a significant turning point in the global commitment to human rights, including the rights of children. In 1948, the Universal Declaration of Human Rights (UDHR) was adopted by the UN General Assembly, affirming the inherent dignity and equal rights of all human beings, including children. Article 25 of the UDHR specifically mentioned the need for special care and assistance for motherhood and childhood.

Building on the momentum of the UDHR, the United Nations General Assembly adopted the Declaration of the Rights of the Child in 1959. This declaration expanded on the principles outlined in the 1924 Geneva Declaration, articulating ten fundamental rights of children, including the right to education, health care, and protection from exploitation and abuse. While not legally binding, the 1959 Declaration set important normative standards and influenced national policies and legislation.

The most significant development in the international legal framework for child rights came with the adoption of the Convention on the Rights of the Child (CRC) by the UN General Assembly on November 20, 1989. The CRC is the most comprehensive and widely ratified international treaty on child rights, with 196 countries as state parties. The CRC outlines a broad range of rights for children, categorized into four main pillars: survival, development, protection, and participation.

The survival rights include the right to life, adequate nutrition, health care, and a safe environment. The development rights encompass the right to education, play, and cultural activities, as well as access to information and opportunities for personal growth. Protection rights address the safeguarding of children from all forms of abuse, neglect, exploitation, and violence. Participation rights recognize the importance of children having a voice in matters that affect them, respecting their views and involving them in decision-making processes appropriate to their age and maturity.

The CRC also established the principle of the "best interests of the child," which requires that the child's welfare be a primary consideration in all actions concerning them. This principle has been instrumental in shaping child-related policies and practices globally. The CRC's implementation is monitored by the Committee on the Rights of the Child, a body of independent experts that reviews periodic reports submitted by state parties and provides recommendations for improvement.

The CRC has inspired the adoption of numerous national laws and policies aimed at protecting and promoting the rights of children. Many countries have established child protection systems, including specialized agencies, helplines, and child-friendly courts, to address issues such as child abuse, trafficking, and exploitation. Education policies have been reformed to ensure free and compulsory primary education for all children, and health initiatives have been launched to improve child and maternal health outcomes.

Despite these significant advancements, challenges remain in the realization of child rights globally. Poverty, armed conflict, displacement, discrimination, and harmful cultural practices continue to impede the fulfillment of children's rights in many parts of the world. Millions of children are still subjected to child labor, forced marriage, female genital mutilation, and other forms of exploitation and violence. Access to quality education and health care remains elusive for many children, particularly those in marginalized and disadvantaged communities.

The global community has recognized the need for continued efforts to address these challenges and promote the rights of children. The adoption of the Sustainable Development Goals (SDGs) by the United Nations in 2015 reflects this commitment. Several SDGs specifically target issues affecting children, such as ending poverty and hunger, ensuring quality education, promoting health and well-being, and achieving gender equality. The SDGs provide a comprehensive framework for addressing the root causes of child rights violations and promoting sustainable development for all children.

In addition to the SDGs, various international initiatives and partnerships have been established to advance child rights. The Global Partnership to End Violence Against Children, launched in 2016, aims to accelerate action to prevent and respond to violence against children. The Every Woman Every Child movement, initiated by the UN Secretary-General in 2010, focuses on improving the health and well-being of women, children, and adolescents. These initiatives bring together governments, civil society organizations, the private sector, and other stakeholders to collaborate on innovative solutions and mobilize resources for child rights.

The role of civil society organizations and advocacy groups remains crucial in the fight for child rights. Organizations such as UNICEF, Save the Children, Plan International, and ChildFund work tirelessly to provide services, advocate for policy changes, and raise awareness about the rights and needs of children. These organizations often operate in challenging environments, providing essential support to children and families affected by conflict, natural disasters, and other emergencies.

Children themselves have also become powerful advocates for their own rights. Youth movements and child-led initiatives have emerged as influential platforms for raising awareness and driving change. The global climate strikes, led by young activists like Greta Thunberg, highlight the growing role of children and adolescents in advocating for issues that affect their future. The recognition of children's right to participate in decision-making processes has empowered them to voice their concerns and contribute to shaping policies and practices that impact their lives.

# Chapter 15: Indigenous Rights

Indigenous rights refer to the collective and individual rights of indigenous peoples to maintain and strengthen their distinct political, legal, economic, social, and cultural institutions, while retaining their rights to participate fully in the life of the state. These rights encompass a broad range of issues, including land and resource rights, cultural preservation, self-determination, and protection from discrimination and exploitation. The recognition and protection of indigenous rights have evolved over centuries, influenced by historical injustices, colonialism, and the persistent advocacy of indigenous communities and their allies.

The historical context of indigenous rights is deeply rooted in the colonial expansion that began in the late 15th century. European colonization led to the dispossession, displacement, and decimation of indigenous populations across the Americas, Africa, Asia, and Oceania. Colonizers imposed their own legal systems, economic structures, and cultural norms, often marginalizing and suppressing indigenous traditions, languages, and governance systems. The consequences of colonialism were devastating, resulting in loss of land, livelihoods, and cultural identity for many indigenous communities.

Despite these adversities, indigenous peoples resisted colonial domination through various means, including armed resistance, legal challenges, and cultural preservation efforts. The resilience and resistance of indigenous communities have been instrumental in the long struggle for recognition and rights. Throughout the 19th and early 20th centuries, indigenous leaders and activists increasingly sought to assert their rights through legal and political channels. This period saw the emergence of indigenous organizations and movements advocating for land rights, political representation, and cultural autonomy.

A significant milestone in the recognition of indigenous rights came with the establishment of the International Labour Organization

(ILO) in 1919. The ILO's Indigenous and Tribal Populations Convention, 1957 (No. 107), was one of the first international treaties to specifically address the rights of indigenous and tribal peoples. The convention aimed to improve the living and working conditions of indigenous peoples, promoting their integration into national economies and societies. However, it was criticized for its assimilationist approach, which failed to fully respect the distinct identities and autonomy of indigenous communities.

The global decolonization movements of the mid-20th century further catalyzed the push for indigenous rights. As former colonies gained independence, indigenous peoples within these new nation-states continued to face discrimination and marginalization. The civil rights movements in various countries, including the United States, Canada, Australia, and New Zealand, highlighted the systemic injustices faced by indigenous populations and called for greater recognition and protection of their rights.

The 1970s marked a significant turning point with the emergence of a more assertive and coordinated global indigenous rights movement. Indigenous leaders from around the world began to organize and collaborate at the international level, advocating for their rights within the framework of the United Nations (UN). The establishment of the UN Working Group on Indigenous Populations in 1982 provided a crucial platform for indigenous voices and concerns to be heard on the global stage. The working group played a pivotal role in drafting the UN Declaration on the Rights of Indigenous Peoples (UNDRIP).

Adopted by the UN General Assembly on September 13, 2007, UNDRIP is a landmark document that sets out the individual and collective rights of indigenous peoples. It recognizes their rights to self-determination, land, territories, resources, cultural heritage, and traditional knowledge. UNDRIP emphasizes the importance of free, prior, and informed consent (FPIC) in decisions affecting indigenous lands and resources, ensuring that indigenous peoples have a say in matters that impact their lives and communities. Although UNDRIP is not legally binding, it provides a comprehensive framework and moral authority for the promotion and protection of indigenous rights globally.

Land and resource rights are central to the struggle for indigenous rights. Indigenous peoples have a profound spiritual and cultural connection to their ancestral lands, which are integral to their identity, livelihoods, and traditional practices. However, the historical dispossession and ongoing encroachment on indigenous lands by states, corporations, and private actors continue to be major issues. Conflicts over land and resources often result in human rights abuses, environmental degradation, and the loss of traditional knowledge and practices.

Various legal and policy mechanisms have been developed to address indigenous land rights. These include land restitution programs, the recognition of indigenous land titles, and the establishment of protected areas managed by indigenous communities. In some countries, courts have played a significant role in upholding indigenous land rights. For example, in Canada, landmark Supreme Court rulings such as Calder v. British Columbia (1973) and Delgamuukw v. British Columbia (1997) have affirmed the existence of indigenous land rights and the duty of the government to consult with indigenous peoples on matters affecting their lands.

Cultural rights are another critical aspect of indigenous rights. Indigenous peoples possess unique languages, traditions, rituals, and ways of life that are vital to their identity and survival. Cultural assimilation policies, such as residential schools in Canada and the United States, sought to eradicate indigenous cultures and languages, causing profound intergenerational trauma. Today, there is a growing recognition of the need to preserve and revitalize indigenous cultures. Efforts to support indigenous language education, protect sacred sites, and promote traditional knowledge and practices are essential for the survival and flourishing of indigenous cultures.

Self-determination is a foundational principle of indigenous rights, enshrined in both UNDRIP and international human rights law. Self-determination recognizes the right of indigenous peoples to freely determine their political status and pursue their economic, social, and cultural development. This principle encompasses a range of rights, including political autonomy, self-governance, and the ability to maintain and develop their own institutions and legal systems. Various models of indigenous self-determination exist, from autonomous regions and self-governing territories to co-management arrangements and participatory governance structures.

The right to self-determination also includes economic rights, such as the ability to manage and benefit from natural resources on indigenous lands. Many indigenous communities have developed sustainable and culturally appropriate economic enterprises, such as eco-tourism, traditional crafts, and community-managed fisheries and forestry projects. These initiatives not only provide economic benefits but also reinforce cultural values and strengthen community cohesion.

The protection of indigenous rights requires addressing systemic discrimination and ensuring access to justice. Indigenous peoples often face significant barriers in accessing legal and administrative systems, which can perpetuate inequality and injustice. Legal reforms, the establishment of indigenous legal services, and the training of judges and lawyers in indigenous rights are crucial for ensuring that indigenous peoples can effectively defend their rights and seek redress for violations.

International and regional human rights bodies play a vital role in monitoring and promoting indigenous rights. The UN Permanent Forum on Indigenous Issues (UNPFII), established in 2000, provides expert advice and recommendations on indigenous issues to the UN system and raises awareness about indigenous rights. The UN Special

Rapporteur on the rights of indigenous peoples investigates and reports on human rights violations against indigenous communities and advocates for their protection and promotion. Regional human rights mechanisms, such as the Inter-American Commission on Human Rights and the African Commission on Human and Peoples' Rights, also address indigenous rights within their respective regions.

The advancement of indigenous rights is closely linked to broader movements for social and environmental justice. Indigenous peoples have been at the forefront of environmental protection, advocating for sustainable development and the conservation of biodiversity. Their traditional knowledge and practices offer valuable insights for addressing global challenges such as climate change and environmental degradation. The recognition of indigenous rights to land and resources is not only a matter of justice but also a critical component of effective environmental stewardship.

Despite significant progress, many challenges remain in the realization of indigenous rights. Discrimination, violence, and marginalization continue to affect indigenous communities worldwide. The implementation of international standards and national laws often falls short, and indigenous peoples frequently face obstacles in accessing their rights and participating in decision-making processes. Ongoing advocacy, solidarity, and collaboration are essential for advancing the rights and well-being of indigenous peoples.

In recent years, there has been a growing recognition of the importance of indigenous leadership and perspectives in addressing global issues. Indigenous leaders, activists, and organizations have increasingly been recognized and included in international forums, policy discussions, and decision-making processes. Their voices and experiences are critical for developing inclusive and sustainable solutions to the complex challenges facing the world today.

The evolution of indigenous rights is a testament to the resilience, strength, and determination of indigenous peoples to defend their identities, lands, and ways of life. It reflects a growing acknowledgment of the injustices they have endured and the need to rectify historical wrongs. The journey towards full recognition and protection of indigenous rights is ongoing, requiring continued vigilance, advocacy, and solidarity. By upholding the rights of indigenous peoples, we not only honor their contributions and heritage but also promote a more just, equitable, and sustainable world for all.

# Chapter 16: Disability Rights

Disability rights refer to the fundamental freedoms and entitlements of individuals with disabilities, aimed at ensuring their full and equal participation in all aspects of society. This encompasses a wide range of issues, including accessibility, employment, education, health care, social inclusion, and protection from discrimination and abuse. The evolution of disability rights has been marked by significant legal, social, and cultural changes, reflecting a growing recognition of the dignity and worth of people with disabilities and the imperative to eliminate barriers to their full inclusion and participation.

Historically, individuals with disabilities were often marginalized, stigmatized, and excluded from mainstream society. Many societies viewed disabilities through a medical or charity lens, focusing on the impairment itself rather than the rights and potential of the person. People with disabilities were frequently institutionalized, denied education, and subjected to various forms of discrimination and abuse. The dominant societal attitudes saw disabilities as conditions to be cured or pitied, rather than recognizing the inherent rights and contributions of individuals with disabilities.

The early 20th century witnessed the beginnings of a shift in attitudes towards disabilities, influenced by broader social and political movements advocating for human rights and social justice. After World War I, many veterans returned home with disabilities, prompting a greater awareness of the need for rehabilitation and support services. This period saw the establishment of organizations dedicated to the welfare of people with disabilities, such as the American Foundation for the Blind (1921) and the National Federation of the Blind (1940) in the United States.

The mid-20th century marked significant progress in the recognition of disability rights, particularly in the context of the broader civil rights movements. The disability rights movement drew inspiration from the struggles of other marginalized groups, such as African Americans and women, advocating for equal rights and opportunities. Activists and organizations began to challenge discriminatory practices and policies, demanding access to education, employment, public services, and the built environment.

A pivotal moment in the disability rights movement was the passage of the Rehabilitation Act of 1973 in the United States. Section 504 of the act was the first federal civil rights law to protect individuals with disabilities from discrimination. It prohibited discrimination in any program or activity receiving federal financial assistance and laid the groundwork for future legislation. The implementation of Section 504 faced significant resistance, leading to a series of protests and sit-ins by disability activists in 1977. These demonstrations, known as the Section 504 Sit-ins, played a crucial role in raising awareness and securing the enforcement of the law.

Building on the momentum of the Rehabilitation Act, the disability rights movement continued to gain traction, culminating in the passage of the Americans with Disabilities Act (ADA) in 1990. The ADA is a landmark civil rights law that prohibits discrimination against individuals with disabilities in all areas of public life, including employment, education, transportation, and public accommodations. The ADA established comprehensive accessibility standards, ensuring that people with disabilities have equal opportunities to participate in society. Its impact has been profound, leading to significant improvements in accessibility and inclusion across the United States.

Internationally, the recognition of disability rights has also advanced significantly over the past few decades. The adoption of the Convention on the Rights of Persons with Disabilities (CRPD) by the United Nations General Assembly on December 13, 2006, marked a watershed moment in the global disability rights movement. The CRPD is the first comprehensive international treaty to specifically address the rights of people with disabilities, emphasizing their inherent dignity, autonomy, and right to full and equal participation in society. The convention has been ratified by over 180 countries, reflecting a broad international consensus on the importance of disability rights.

The CRPD outlines a wide range of rights for people with disabilities, including the right to accessibility, independent living, education, health care, employment, and participation in political and public life. It also highlights the importance of combating stereotypes, prejudices, and harmful practices related to disability. The principle of "reasonable accommodation" is central to the CRPD, requiring states to make necessary adjustments and modifications to ensure that individuals with disabilities can enjoy their rights on an equal basis with others. The CRPD also established the Committee on the Rights of Persons with Disabilities, a body of independent experts responsible for monitoring the implementation of the convention and providing guidance to state parties.

The recognition of disability rights has led to significant legal and policy reforms in many countries. National laws and policies have been enacted to promote accessibility, protect against discrimination, and ensure the inclusion of people with disabilities in various aspects of society. These reforms have been accompanied by efforts to raise awareness and change societal attitudes towards disabilities, promoting a more inclusive and accepting environment.

Accessibility is a fundamental aspect of disability rights, encompassing physical, digital, and informational accessibility. Ensuring that buildings, transportation systems, and public spaces are accessible to people with disabilities is crucial for their independence and participation in society. This includes features such as ramps, elevators, accessible restrooms, and tactile paving for individuals with visual impairments. Digital accessibility involves making websites, software, and digital content usable by people with disabilities, including those with visual, auditory, cognitive, and motor impairments. The Web Content Accessibility Guidelines (WCAG), developed by the World Wide Web Consortium (W3C), provide a set of standards for creating accessible digital content.

Employment is another critical area where disability rights have made significant strides. People with disabilities have historically faced high rates of unemployment and underemployment, often due to discriminatory practices and lack of accommodations in the workplace. Laws such as the ADA and the CRPD require employers to provide reasonable accommodations and prohibit discrimination based on disability. These measures have led to greater inclusion of people with disabilities in the workforce, enabling them to contribute their skills and talents to the economy.

Education is a key determinant of opportunities and outcomes for people with disabilities. Inclusive education, which involves integrating students with disabilities into mainstream schools and classrooms, is widely recognized as the best practice for promoting equality and social inclusion. The Individuals with Disabilities Education Act (IDEA) in the United States and similar laws in other countries mandate that students with disabilities have access to free and appropriate public education in the least restrictive environment. Inclusive education benefits not only students with disabilities but also their peers, fostering a more diverse and accepting learning environment.

Health care is another essential area where disability rights are crucial. People with disabilities often face barriers to accessing health care services, including physical inaccessibility, lack of trained health care providers, and discriminatory attitudes. Ensuring that health care services are accessible and responsive to the needs of people with disabilities is vital for their well-being and quality of life. This includes providing accessible medical facilities, training health care providers on disability issues, and addressing the specific health care needs of people with disabilities.

Social inclusion and participation are fundamental to the realization of disability rights. People with disabilities have the right to participate fully in cultural, recreational, and community activities. This includes access to sports, arts, and cultural events, as well as opportunities for social interaction and community engagement. Efforts to promote social inclusion involve removing barriers, creating inclusive spaces, and fostering positive attitudes towards people with disabilities.

Despite significant progress, challenges remain in the realization of disability rights. People with disabilities continue to face discrimination, stigma, and exclusion in many parts of the world. Access to education, employment, health care, and social services remains limited for many individuals with disabilities, particularly in low- and middle-income countries. The COVID-19 pandemic has exacerbated these challenges, highlighting the vulnerabilities and inequities faced by people with disabilities.

Advancing disability rights requires ongoing advocacy, policy reforms, and societal change. Disability rights organizations and activists play a crucial role in raising awareness, advocating for legal and policy changes, and supporting individuals with disabilities. International organizations, such as the World Health Organization (WHO) and the International Disability Alliance (IDA), work to promote disability rights and support the implementation of the CRPD globally.

The recognition and protection of disability rights are essential for building inclusive, equitable, and just societies. People with disabilities have the right to live with dignity, autonomy, and full participation in all aspects of life. By ensuring that disability rights are respected and upheld, we not only improve the lives of individuals with disabilities but also enrich our communities and societies as a whole. The journey towards the full realization of disability rights is ongoing, requiring continued commitment, collaboration, and action to create a world where everyone can thrive.

# Chapter 17: Refugee Protections

Refugee protections encompass a complex and multifaceted array of international legal frameworks, national policies, and humanitarian efforts designed to safeguard the rights and well-being of individuals who flee their home countries due to persecution, conflict, or violence. This detailed exploration will cover the historical development of refugee protections, the legal instruments and principles governing refugee status, the roles of international organizations and states, the challenges faced by refugees, and contemporary issues impacting refugee protections.

The concept of providing refuge to those fleeing persecution is ancient, with roots in various cultures and religions. However, the modern system of refugee protections began to take shape in the early 20th century, in response to the massive displacement caused by wars and political upheavals. The League of Nations, established after World War I, created the first international agreements and mechanisms for protecting refugees. In 1921, Fridtjof Nansen, a Norwegian explorer and diplomat, was appointed as the League's High Commissioner for Refugees. He initiated the issuance of "Nansen passports," which allowed stateless refugees to travel and settle in new countries.

The atrocities of World War II and the subsequent displacement of millions of people highlighted the need for a more comprehensive and robust international framework. In 1951, the United Nations adopted the Convention relating to the Status of Refugees, often referred to as the 1951 Refugee Convention. This convention, along with its 1967 Protocol, forms the cornerstone of international refugee law. The 1951 Refugee Convention defines who qualifies as a refugee, outlines their rights, and sets out the legal obligations of states to protect them.

According to the 1951 Refugee Convention, a refugee is someone who, owing to a well-founded fear of persecution for reasons of race, religion, nationality, membership of a particular social group, or political opinion, is outside their country of nationality and is unable or unwilling to avail themselves of the protection of that country. This definition encompasses several key elements: the existence of a well-founded fear of persecution, the basis for persecution, and the inability or unwillingness to seek protection from one's home country.

One of the fundamental principles of the 1951 Refugee Convention is non-refoulement, which prohibits the expulsion or return of a refugee to a territory where their life or freedom would be threatened. This principle is considered a cornerstone of international refugee protection and is binding on all states, regardless of whether they have ratified the 1951 Convention or its 1967 Protocol. Non-refoulement ensures that refugees are not forcibly returned to places where they face serious harm, thereby providing a critical safeguard for their safety and security.

The 1951 Refugee Convention also establishes the rights of refugees, which include the right to work, access to education, freedom of movement, and protection from discrimination and arbitrary detention. These rights are intended to facilitate the integration and self-sufficiency of refugees in their host countries. The convention also obliges states to cooperate with the United Nations High Commissioner for Refugees (UNHCR), the primary international body responsible for coordinating refugee protection and assistance.

The UNHCR, established in 1950, plays a pivotal role in the global refugee protection regime. Its mandate includes providing international protection to refugees, seeking durable solutions to their plight, and assisting in the voluntary repatriation, local integration, or resettlement of refugees. The UNHCR works in collaboration with governments, non-governmental organizations (NGOs), and other international agencies to deliver humanitarian aid, advocate for refugee rights, and develop policies and programs that support refugees.

Durable solutions for refugees typically involve three main options: voluntary repatriation, local integration, and resettlement.

Voluntary repatriation occurs when refugees return to their home countries when conditions have improved to ensure their safety and dignity. Local integration involves the granting of legal status, rights, and opportunities for refugees to become self-reliant and integrated into the host country's society. Resettlement involves the transfer of refugees from an asylum country to another state that agrees to admit them and provide permanent settlement. Each of these solutions presents unique challenges and requires coordinated efforts from the international community.

The global refugee crisis has grown significantly in recent years, driven by conflicts, persecution, and human rights abuses in various regions. As of the end of 2020, the UNHCR reported that there were over 26 million refugees worldwide, with the majority originating from countries such as Syria, Afghanistan, South Sudan, Myanmar, and Somalia. The displacement crisis has placed immense pressure on host countries, many of which are developing nations with limited resources and infrastructure to support large refugee populations.

One of the major challenges in refugee protection is the burden-sharing among states. While some countries, particularly those in Europe and North America, have well-established asylum systems and resources to support refugees, others, often neighboring conflict zones, bear a disproportionate share of the refugee burden. Countries such as Turkey, Lebanon, Jordan, and Uganda host millions of refugees, often with limited international assistance and support. This imbalance has led to calls for greater international cooperation and equitable burden-sharing to ensure that all countries contribute to the global effort to protect refugees.

The resettlement of refugees to third countries is a vital component of the international refugee protection system, providing a solution for those who cannot return home or integrate locally. However, the number of resettlement places available globally is far below the need. In recent years, the United States, Canada, and several European countries have been the primary destinations for resettled refugees. However, resettlement programs have faced challenges, including restrictive immigration policies, security concerns, and limited political will, resulting in a decline in the number of refugees being resettled.

The integration of refugees into host communities presents another significant challenge. Refugees often face numerous barriers, including language difficulties, cultural differences, discrimination, and limited access to education and employment opportunities. Successful integration requires comprehensive support systems, including language and vocational training, access to social services, and initiatives to promote social cohesion and combat xenophobia. Host communities also play a crucial role in the integration process, as positive attitudes and inclusive policies can significantly enhance refugees' ability to rebuild their lives and contribute to their new societies.

Women and children constitute a significant proportion of the global refugee population and face specific protection challenges. Refugee women are particularly vulnerable to gender-based violence, exploitation, and discrimination. Ensuring their protection requires targeted interventions, including safe shelter, access to sexual and reproductive health services, and legal support. Refugee children, many of whom are unaccompanied or separated from their families, require special protection and assistance to address their unique needs. This includes access to education, psychosocial support, and family reunification efforts.

The protection of refugees with disabilities is another critical issue that requires attention. Refugees with disabilities face heightened risks of discrimination, exclusion, and barriers to accessing essential services. Ensuring their inclusion in refugee protection and assistance programs involves addressing physical, communication, and attitudinal barriers, providing appropriate support services, and promoting their participation in decision-making processes.

In addition to traditional refugee protection challenges, contemporary issues such as climate change and environmental displacement are increasingly impacting refugee protection efforts. Climate change exacerbates existing vulnerabilities and can lead to displacement due to extreme weather events, sea-level rise, and environmental degradation. While those displaced by environmental factors do not typically fall under the 1951 Refugee Convention's definition, there is growing recognition of the need to address their protection needs through legal and policy frameworks.

Efforts to enhance refugee protections also involve addressing the root causes of displacement, including conflict, persecution, and human rights abuses. Sustainable peacebuilding, conflict resolution, and development initiatives are essential to create conditions conducive to the voluntary return of refugees and the prevention of future displacement. The international community must also address the structural inequalities and power dynamics that contribute to displacement and hinder the protection of refugees.

International and regional organizations play a crucial role in advancing refugee protections. The UNHCR, as the leading agency for refugee protection, works in collaboration with other UN agencies, such as the International Organization for Migration (IOM), UNICEF, and the World Food Programme (WFP), to provide comprehensive support to refugees. Regional bodies, such as the African Union (AU) and the European Union (EU), have also developed frameworks and mechanisms to address refugee protection within their respective regions.

The role of civil society organizations, including NGOs, community-based organizations, and faith-based groups, is vital in supporting refugees and advocating for their rights. These organizations often provide essential services, including legal assistance, healthcare, education, and psychosocial support, and play a key role in raising awareness and mobilizing public support for refugee protection.

The protection of refugees is a shared global responsibility that requires a concerted and coordinated effort from all stakeholders, including states, international organizations, civil society, and host communities. The principles of humanity, solidarity, and respect for human rights must guide our actions to ensure that refugees receive the protection and support they need to rebuild their lives in safety and dignity.

The evolution of refugee protections reflects a journey marked by significant achievements and ongoing challenges. From the early efforts of the League of Nations to the establishment of the UNHCR and the adoption of the 1951 Refugee Convention, the international community has made substantial progress in recognizing and upholding the rights of refugees. However, the increasing scale and complexity of displacement crises demand continued commitment, innovation, and collaboration to address the protection needs of refugees effectively. By upholding the principles of refugee protection and working towards durable solutions, we can create a more just, compassionate, and inclusive world for all.

# Chapter 18: Digital Rights

Digital rights refer to the human rights and freedoms that individuals have in the digital world, encompassing a broad spectrum of issues including privacy, freedom of expression, access to information, data protection, and the right to be free from digital surveillance. As the internet and digital technologies have become integral to nearly every aspect of modern life, the importance of digital rights has grown exponentially. The concept of digital rights intersects with traditional human rights, extending them into the digital realm and addressing new challenges posed by the proliferation of digital technologies. This exploration will delve deeply into the evolution, legal frameworks, key issues, and contemporary debates surrounding digital rights.

The origins of digital rights can be traced back to the early days of the internet, a time when the digital landscape was rapidly expanding but largely unregulated. In the 1990s, as the internet began to transform communication, commerce, and information sharing, it became apparent that existing legal frameworks were insufficient to address the unique challenges posed by digital technologies. Early digital rights advocates, such as the Electronic Frontier Foundation (EFF), founded in 1990, began to champion the protection of civil liberties in the digital world. They argued that the principles of free speech, privacy, and due process must be preserved online as they are offline.

One of the foundational legal frameworks for digital rights is the Universal Declaration of Human Rights (UDHR), adopted by the United Nations General Assembly in 1948. Although the UDHR does not explicitly address digital rights, its principles have been interpreted to apply to the digital age. For instance, Article 19 of the UDHR, which guarantees the right to freedom of opinion and expression, has been extended to include online expression. Similarly, Article 12, which protects individuals from arbitrary interference with their privacy, is foundational for digital privacy rights.

The Council of Europe's Convention for the Protection of Human Rights and Fundamental Freedoms (European Convention on Human Rights), adopted in 1950, also plays a crucial role in shaping digital rights, particularly in Europe. The European Court of Human Rights (ECHR) has adjudicated numerous cases involving digital rights issues, including privacy, surveillance, and freedom of expression online. The court's rulings have significantly influenced the development of digital rights jurisprudence.

A major milestone in the evolution of digital rights was the adoption of the General Data Protection Regulation (GDPR) by the European Union in 2016. The GDPR represents one of the most comprehensive data protection laws in the world, establishing strict rules for how personal data must be handled by organizations. Key principles of the GDPR include the requirement for explicit consent for data processing, the right to access and rectify personal data, the right to data portability, and the right to erasure (also known as the "right to be forgotten"). The GDPR has set a global standard for data protection and has influenced similar legislation in other regions.

Privacy is one of the central pillars of digital rights. In the digital age, vast amounts of personal data are collected, processed, and stored by governments, corporations, and other entities. This data can include sensitive information such as medical records, financial details, location data, and online activities. Protecting this data from unauthorized access, misuse, and exploitation is critical to safeguarding individuals' privacy. Privacy rights in the digital realm encompass the right to control one's personal information, the right to be informed about data collection and processing practices, and the right to secure and private communications.

The right to privacy is increasingly challenged by the practices of mass surveillance and data mining. Governments and intelligence agencies often justify surveillance programs on the grounds of national security and crime prevention. However, these practices can infringe upon individuals' privacy and civil liberties. Revelations by whistleblowers such as Edward Snowden have highlighted the extensive surveillance activities conducted by agencies like the U.S. National Security Agency (NSA), sparking global debates about the balance between security and privacy. Legal frameworks such as the GDPR, the U.S. Electronic Communications Privacy Act (ECPA), and the International Covenant on Civil and Political Rights (ICCPR) aim to provide protections against unwarranted surveillance, though their effectiveness varies by jurisdiction.

Another critical aspect of digital rights is freedom of expression. The internet has transformed how people communicate, share ideas, and engage in public discourse. It provides a platform for diverse voices and has democratized access to information and expression. However, digital platforms also pose challenges to freedom of expression, including censorship, content moderation, and the spread of misinformation. Governments, social media companies, and other entities often grapple with the complex task of balancing free speech with the need to prevent harm, such as hate speech, violence, and misinformation.

Censorship and content regulation on digital platforms are contentious issues. Authoritarian regimes often use internet censorship to suppress dissent, control information, and silence opposition. Techniques such as internet shutdowns, blocking websites, and surveillance are commonly employed to restrict digital freedoms. In democratic societies, content moderation by private companies, such as social media platforms, raises questions about the role of these entities in regulating speech. Platforms like Facebook, Twitter, and YouTube have developed policies and algorithms to remove harmful content, but these measures can sometimes result in overreach and the suppression of legitimate expression.

The spread of misinformation and disinformation online has emerged as a significant challenge to digital rights and democratic processes. False information can spread rapidly on social media, influencing public opinion and undermining trust in institutions. Addressing this issue requires a multifaceted approach, including media literacy education, fact-checking initiatives, and transparent content moderation practices. However, efforts to combat misinformation must be carefully balanced to avoid infringing upon free speech.

Access to information is another fundamental digital right. The internet provides unprecedented opportunities for accessing and sharing information, which is essential for education, innovation, and participation in democratic processes. However, the digital divide – the gap between those who have access to digital technologies and those who do not – remains a significant barrier to realizing this right. Factors such as socioeconomic status, geography, and infrastructure contribute to unequal access to the internet and digital resources. Bridging the digital divide requires investment in digital infrastructure, affordable internet services, and digital literacy programs to ensure that everyone can benefit from the opportunities afforded by the digital age.

Data protection is closely linked to privacy rights and involves safeguarding personal data from unauthorized access, use, and disclosure. The GDPR and similar laws provide comprehensive frameworks for data protection, but challenges remain in enforcing these regulations and ensuring compliance. Data breaches, cyberattacks, and unauthorized data sharing are persistent threats to data security. Companies and organizations that collect and process personal data must implement robust security measures and adhere to best practices to protect data integrity and confidentiality.

Digital rights also encompass issues of digital identity and autonomy. Individuals should have control over their digital identities, including how their data is used and shared. The concept of digital self-determination emphasizes the right to make informed choices about one's digital presence and the use of personal data. This includes the ability to access, correct, and delete personal information, as well as the right to consent to data processing activities. Digital identity management systems, such as blockchain-based solutions, are being explored as ways to enhance privacy and security while giving individuals greater control over their digital identities.

The right to be forgotten, enshrined in the GDPR, allows individuals to request the removal of their personal data from online platforms and search engines. This right aims to protect individuals' privacy and reputations by allowing them to manage their digital footprints. However, implementing the right to be forgotten raises complex legal and ethical questions, particularly regarding the balance between privacy and the public's right to access information.

Digital rights are also relevant in the context of emerging technologies such as artificial intelligence (AI), machine learning, and big data analytics. These technologies have the potential to transform society, but they also pose significant risks to privacy, autonomy, and equality. AI systems can perpetuate biases, make opaque decisions, and impact individuals' rights in various domains, including employment, healthcare, and criminal justice. Ensuring that AI and other emerging technologies are developed and deployed in ways that respect human rights requires robust ethical guidelines, transparency, accountability, and regulatory oversight.

The intersection of digital rights with intellectual property (IP) is another area of concern. The protection of IP rights, such as copyright and patents, must be balanced with the rights to access information and freedom of expression. The digital environment has transformed the way content is created, distributed, and consumed, leading to debates about the enforcement of IP rights online. Issues such as digital rights management (DRM), fair use, and the sharing of digital content require careful consideration to ensure that IP protections do not unduly restrict digital freedoms.

International cooperation and multilateral frameworks are essential for advancing digital rights. The United Nations and other international bodies play crucial roles in promoting and protecting digital rights through initiatives such as the UN Guiding Principles on Business and Human Rights and the work of the UN Special Rapporteur on the right to privacy. Regional organizations, such as the European Union and the Council of Europe, have developed specific regulations and standards to protect digital rights within their jurisdictions. Global forums, such as the Internet Governance Forum (IGF), provide platforms for dialogue and collaboration among governments, civil society, the private sector, and other stakeholders on digital rights issues.

Civil society organizations, advocacy groups, and digital rights activists are instrumental in defending and promoting digital rights. Organizations like the EFF, Access Now, Privacy International, and the Center for Democracy and Technology (CDT) work tirelessly to raise awareness, influence policy, and provide legal support to individuals and communities affected by digital rights violations. Grassroots movements and campaigns, such as the fight against mass surveillance and the advocacy for net neutrality, demonstrate the power of collective action in shaping digital rights.

# Chapter 19: Environmental Rights

Environmental rights refer to the entitlements and protections related to the environment that ensure individuals and communities can live in a healthy, safe, and sustainable environment. These rights encompass a wide range of issues including the right to clean air and water, the right to access natural resources, the right to live in a non-toxic environment, and the right to participate in environmental decision-making processes. The concept of environmental rights has evolved significantly over the past few decades, driven by growing awareness of environmental issues, legal developments, and the recognition of the intrinsic link between human rights and environmental health. This detailed exploration will cover the historical evolution of environmental rights, the legal frameworks and principles underpinning these rights, key issues and challenges, and contemporary debates and developments in the field.

The historical development of environmental rights is closely tied to the broader environmental movement that emerged in the mid-20th century. Before this period, environmental concerns were often secondary to economic and industrial development. However, the rapid industrialization and urbanization of the 20th century led to widespread environmental degradation, prompting a shift in public consciousness. Landmark events such as the publication of Rachel Carson's "Silent Spring" in 1962, which highlighted the dangers of pesticide use, and the first Earth Day in 1970, which mobilized millions of people in support of environmental protection, played crucial roles in raising awareness about the importance of environmental health.

The 1972 United Nations Conference on the Human Environment, held in Stockholm, marked a significant milestone in the recognition of environmental rights at the international level. The conference resulted in the Stockholm Declaration, which proclaimed that humans have the fundamental right to "freedom, equality, and adequate conditions of life, in an environment of a quality that permits a life of dignity and well-being." This declaration laid the groundwork for integrating environmental concerns into the human rights framework and set the stage for future international agreements and initiatives.

Following the Stockholm Conference, numerous international treaties and conventions were adopted to address specific environmental issues. The United Nations Environment Programme (UNEP) was established in 1972 to coordinate global environmental efforts. The 1987 Brundtland Report, officially titled "Our Common Future," introduced the concept of sustainable development, emphasizing the need to balance environmental protection, economic growth, and social equity. The report underscored that environmental degradation could undermine the fulfillment of human rights, particularly for marginalized and vulnerable communities.

The 1992 United Nations Conference on Environment and Development (UNCED), also known as the Earth Summit, held in Rio de Janeiro, further advanced the global environmental agenda. The Earth Summit produced several key documents, including the Rio Declaration on Environment and Development, Agenda 21, and the Convention on Biological Diversity (CBD). The Rio Declaration reaffirmed the right to a healthy environment and emphasized the principle of sustainable development. It also introduced the concept of common but differentiated responsibilities, recognizing that developed and developing countries have different capacities and responsibilities in addressing environmental challenges.

The Aarhus Convention, adopted in 1998 by the United Nations Economic Commission for Europe (UNECE), represents a significant development in the recognition and implementation of environmental rights. Formally known as the Convention on Access to Information, Public Participation in Decision-Making, and Access to Justice in

Environmental Matters, the Aarhus Convention establishes procedural rights related to the environment. These include the right to access environmental information, the right to participate in environmental decision-making processes, and the right to seek legal redress for environmental harm. The convention underscores the importance of transparency, accountability, and public participation in environmental governance.

Environmental rights are grounded in several key principles that guide their interpretation and implementation. These principles include the precautionary principle, the polluter pays principle, the principle of intergenerational equity, and the principle of sustainable development. The precautionary principle asserts that when there is a risk of significant harm to the environment or human health, the absence of complete scientific certainty should not be used as a reason for postponing measures to prevent environmental degradation. The polluter pays principle holds that those responsible for causing pollution or environmental harm should bear the costs of managing and mitigating its impacts. The principle of intergenerational equity emphasizes that present generations have a responsibility to manage natural resources in a way that does not compromise the ability of future generations to meet their own needs. The principle of sustainable development seeks to balance environmental protection, economic growth, and social well-being.

The legal recognition of environmental rights varies across different jurisdictions, with some countries enshrining these rights in their constitutions and legal frameworks. For example, the Constitution of Ecuador, adopted in 2008, recognizes the rights of nature, granting ecosystems the right to exist, flourish, and evolve. Similarly, the Constitution of South Africa includes a provision that guarantees everyone the right to an environment that is not harmful to their health or well-being and mandates the state to take measures to protect the environment for present and future generations. Other countries, such as Norway and Finland, have also incorporated environmental rights into their constitutions, reflecting a growing recognition of the fundamental importance of environmental protection.

One of the critical challenges in realizing environmental rights is the issue of environmental justice. Environmental justice addresses the disproportionate impact of environmental degradation on marginalized and vulnerable communities, including low-income populations, indigenous peoples, and communities of color. These groups often bear the brunt of pollution, hazardous waste, and other environmental hazards due to systemic inequalities and discriminatory practices. Environmental justice advocates seek to ensure that all people have equal access to a healthy environment and that the benefits and burdens of environmental policies are distributed equitably.

Climate change represents one of the most pressing challenges to environmental rights in the contemporary era. The impacts of climate change, including rising temperatures, sea-level rise, extreme weather events, and shifts in ecosystems, pose significant threats to human rights, including the rights to life, health, food, water, and shelter. Vulnerable communities, particularly those in developing countries and small island states, are disproportionately affected by climate change despite contributing the least to global greenhouse gas emissions. International efforts to address climate change, such as the Paris Agreement adopted in 2015, aim to limit global warming and promote climate resilience. However, achieving these goals requires concerted action and cooperation from all countries, as well as the integration of human rights considerations into climate policies and strategies.

Water rights are another crucial aspect of environmental rights, as access to clean and safe water is essential for human health and well-being. The right to water is recognized as a fundamental human right by the United Nations, and ensuring access to safe drinking water and sanitation is a key target of the Sustainable Development Goals

(SDGs). However, water scarcity, pollution, and inadequate infrastructure continue to pose significant challenges in many parts of the world. Effective water management and governance are essential to protect water resources and ensure equitable access for all.

Biodiversity and ecosystem protection are integral to the realization of environmental rights, as healthy ecosystems provide essential services that support human life and livelihoods. The loss of biodiversity due to habitat destruction, pollution, overexploitation, and climate change threatens the stability and resilience of ecosystems. International agreements such as the Convention on Biological Diversity (CBD) aim to conserve biodiversity, promote sustainable use of biological resources, and ensure the fair and equitable sharing of benefits arising from genetic resources. Protecting biodiversity and ecosystems requires collaborative efforts at the local, national, and global levels, as well as the recognition and respect of indigenous and local communities' traditional knowledge and practices.

Air quality is another critical component of environmental rights, as air pollution poses severe health risks and contributes to environmental degradation. The right to breathe clean air is increasingly recognized as a fundamental human right, with legal frameworks and policies aimed at reducing air pollution and mitigating its impacts. Sources of air pollution include industrial emissions, vehicle exhaust, agricultural activities, and household burning of solid fuels. Addressing air pollution requires stringent regulations, monitoring, and enforcement, as well as public awareness and engagement.

The rights of indigenous peoples are closely intertwined with environmental rights, as indigenous communities often have deep cultural, spiritual, and economic connections to their ancestral lands and natural resources. The United Nations Declaration on the Rights of Indigenous Peoples (UNDRIP), adopted in 2007, affirms the rights of indigenous peoples to their traditional lands, territories, and resources, as well as their right to participate in environmental decision-making processes. Respecting and upholding the rights of indigenous peoples is essential for achieving environmental justice and sustainable development, as indigenous knowledge and practices play a vital role in biodiversity conservation and ecosystem management.

Environmental defenders, individuals, and communities who advocate for the protection of the environment and human rights, often face significant risks and threats. Environmental defenders may be subject to harassment, intimidation, violence, and even murder, particularly in contexts where powerful interests are at stake. Protecting environmental defenders and ensuring their ability to carry out their work safely and effectively is crucial for advancing environmental rights. International mechanisms, such as the United Nations Special Rapporteur on the situation of human rights defenders, play a vital role in monitoring and addressing threats to environmental defenders.

Contemporary debates in the field of environmental rights include the recognition of ecocide as an international crime. Ecocide refers to widespread, severe, or systematic damage to the environment, and there is growing support for its inclusion as a crime under international law, akin to genocide and crimes against humanity. Recognizing ecocide would hold individuals and entities accountable for significant environmental harm and strengthen legal mechanisms for environmental protection.

The concept of the rights of nature, which recognizes that natural entities such as rivers, forests, and mountains have intrinsic rights, is gaining traction globally. This approach challenges the traditional anthropocentric view of environmental protection and promotes a more holistic and interconnected understanding of the relationship between humans and the environment. Several countries and jurisdictions have adopted legal frameworks recognizing the rights of nature, including Ecuador, Bolivia, and certain municipalities in the United States and New Zealand. These legal innovations aim to provide stronger protections for natural ecosystems and promote sustainable and harmonious coexistence between humans and the environment.

Environmental rights also intersect with other social and economic rights, such as the right to health, the right to housing, and the right to food. Environmental degradation can have profound impacts on these rights, exacerbating health issues, displacing communities, and threatening food security. Integrating environmental considerations into social and economic policies is essential for promoting holistic and sustainable development.

# Chapter 20: Global Human Rights

Global human rights represent a universal framework designed to protect individuals' fundamental freedoms and dignity across all cultures, nations, and regions. The concept of human rights is based on the idea that every person inherently possesses certain rights simply by being human, regardless of nationality, ethnicity, gender, religion, or any other status. These rights are enshrined in various international treaties, conventions, declarations, and organizations dedicated to ensuring their protection and promotion worldwide.

The origins of modern human rights can be traced back to philosophical, religious, and legal traditions that emphasized the inherent worth of individuals. However, the codification of human rights in a global context primarily began in the aftermath of World War II. The atrocities committed during the war, particularly the Holocaust, galvanized the international community to establish a comprehensive set of standards aimed at preventing such horrors from recurring. This led to the formation of the United Nations (UN) in 1945, a pivotal moment in the global human rights movement.

One of the UN's first major achievements was the adoption of the Universal Declaration of Human Rights (UDHR) on December 10, 1948. Drafted by representatives from diverse legal and cultural backgrounds, the UDHR set forth a broad range of rights and freedoms to which all people are entitled. These include civil and political rights, such as the right to life, liberty, and security of person, freedom from torture and arbitrary arrest, and freedom of thought, conscience, and religion. It also encompasses economic, social, and cultural rights, including the right to work, education, and an adequate standard of living.

The UDHR, though not legally binding, has profoundly influenced international law and national constitutions, serving as a foundational text for subsequent human rights treaties and declarations. Over the decades, numerous international human rights instruments have been adopted, building on the principles of the UDHR. Some of the most significant include the International Covenant on Civil and Political Rights (ICCPR) and the International Covenant on Economic, Social, and Cultural Rights (ICESCR), both adopted in 1966. Together with the UDHR, these covenants form the International Bill of Human Rights, establishing a comprehensive legal framework for the protection of a wide array of human rights.

In addition to these broad treaties, there are numerous other international and regional human rights instruments addressing specific issues and groups. For example, the Convention on the Elimination of All Forms of Discrimination Against Women (CEDAW) and the Convention on the Rights of the Child (CRC) specifically protect the rights of women and children, respectively. Other significant treaties include the Convention on the Elimination of All Forms of Racial Discrimination (CERD) and the Convention Against Torture and Other Cruel, Inhuman or Degrading Treatment or Punishment (CAT). These treaties are overseen by various committees and monitoring bodies that review compliance and address violations.

Regional human rights systems also play a crucial role in promoting and protecting human rights. These include the European Convention on Human Rights (ECHR), overseen by the European Court of Human Rights, the American Convention on Human Rights, under the jurisdiction of the Inter-American Court of Human Rights, and the African Charter on Human and Peoples' Rights, enforced by the African Court on Human and Peoples' Rights. These regional mechanisms provide additional layers of protection and accountability, allowing individuals to seek redress for human rights violations when national systems fail.

The enforcement and promotion of global human rights involve a complex interplay of international, regional, and national actors. The

UN Human Rights Council, established in 2006, plays a central role in addressing human rights violations and promoting universal respect for human rights. It conducts periodic reviews of member states' human rights records, investigates specific issues, and responds to emergencies. Additionally, the Office of the High Commissioner for Human Rights (OHCHR) works to strengthen human rights mechanisms, support governments in their obligations, and ensure that human rights are integrated into all aspects of the UN's work.

Non-governmental organizations (NGOs) and civil society groups are also pivotal in the global human rights landscape. Organizations such as Amnesty International, Human Rights Watch, and the International Federation for Human Rights (FIDH) conduct research, advocate for victims, and apply pressure on governments and international bodies to uphold human rights standards. These groups often work on the ground, providing direct assistance to those affected by human rights abuses and raising awareness about violations.

Despite the robust framework and numerous advancements, the global human rights landscape faces significant challenges. Persistent issues such as armed conflict, authoritarian regimes, poverty, discrimination, and climate change continue to undermine human rights worldwide. In many regions, human rights defenders and journalists face harassment, imprisonment, and even death for their work. Additionally, there are growing concerns about the impact of technology on human rights, including privacy violations, surveillance, and the spread of misinformation.

The international community must continually adapt and respond to these evolving challenges. Efforts to strengthen accountability mechanisms, promote inclusive and participatory governance, and address root causes of human rights abuses are essential. Education and awareness-raising about human rights are also crucial in fostering a culture of respect and understanding.

Moreover, the principle of universality, a cornerstone of the human rights framework, sometimes encounters resistance due to cultural, religious, and political differences. Balancing respect for cultural diversity with the imperative to uphold universal human rights standards remains a complex and ongoing task. Dialogues and cooperation between different cultures and societies are vital in finding common ground and advancing human rights globally.

# Epilogue

As we reach the conclusion of "The Progression of Human Rights: From Magna Carta to Modern Movements," it is evident that the journey of human rights is an ongoing and dynamic process. From the early assertions of liberty and justice to the complex challenges of our modern era, the evolution of human rights reflects humanity's enduring quest for dignity, equality, and freedom.

Throughout this book, we have explored significant milestones that have shaped the landscape of human rights. The Magna Carta's groundbreaking principles of limited power and individual rights laid a crucial foundation. The Enlightenment's bold ideas about reason and equality propelled forward movements for independence and democracy. The abolition of slavery, the expansion of suffrage, and the fight for civil rights marked crucial victories in the battle against systemic injustice.

As we moved through the 20th and into the 21st century, the global community embraced a broader understanding of human rights. The Universal Declaration of Human Rights provided a comprehensive framework, inspiring nations to commit to safeguarding these rights for all people. Movements advocating for the rights of children, indigenous peoples, and persons with disabilities expanded our definition of justice and inclusion.

The modern era brings its own set of challenges and opportunities. Digital rights and privacy concerns arise in a world increasingly interconnected by technology. Environmental rights underscore the vital relationship between human well-being and the health of our planet. The plight of refugees and displaced persons demands our compassion and action in addressing humanitarian crises.

Despite significant progress, the work of securing human rights is far from complete. Persistent inequalities, discrimination, and injustices remind us that the fight for human rights requires constant vigilance and advocacy. The victories of the past provide both inspiration and a blueprint for addressing the issues of the present and future.

This epilogue is not an end but a call to action. It is a reminder that each generation must carry the torch of human rights forward, challenging injustices and striving for a world where every individual can live with dignity, freedom, and equality. The stories and movements chronicled in this book illustrate the power of collective action and the impact of unwavering commitment to justice.

As we close these pages, let us remember that the spirit of human rights lives within each of us. Whether through small acts of kindness, bold activism, or systemic change, we all have a role in shaping a just and equitable world. The journey of human rights continues, and it is up to us to write the next chapters, ensuring that the legacy of progress endures and flourishes.

Thank you for joining this exploration of humanity's relentless pursuit of justice. May we all be inspired to contribute to the ongoing evolution of human rights, championing the values of dignity, equality, and freedom for all.


The End.